THE ART OF JOINING: DESIGNING THE UNIVERSAL CONNECTOR

SPECTOR BOOKS

CONTENT

The Art of Joining: Designing the Universal Connector

Edited by Phillip Denny and Adam Przywara

The Biennale Architettura 2018 in Venice took "Freespace" as its theme. As a historic reference to the design of free spaces, Swiss architects Christian Sumi and Marianne Burkhalter and others reconstructed Konrad Wachsmann's "grapevine structures" for the exhibition. Here, they were less concerned with updating the structural innovations that made these spaces possible than with the power of imagination that these vast structures can bring to rethinking the built environment. Today these architectural utopias indebted to technological progress are gaining renewed attention, not only because of their pioneering contribution to digital information architecture, but also because they evoke fundamental questions about the definition of architecture, its knowledge and self-image.

At the heart of these structures that overcome the forces of gravity and monumentality of the building was a connector designed by Konrad Wachsmann to perfect architectonic production. In his book *The Turning Point of Building*, published in the USA in 1959, he showcased a number of such vast lightweight structures.

The book is a programmatic treatise on industrial construction. The arguments it puts forward in words and images evince little interest in an architecture of enclosed volumes and solid structures. Instead, it is structured as a historic narrative of lightweight constructions and supporting structures. Wachsmann sees London's Crystal Palace as a "visible turning point [...] through which the entire development of building history started on a new course".[1]

The structures for telephone masts and observation towers of the inventor of the telephone Alexander Graham Bell likewise provide Wachsmann with arguments in favor of an evolution of technologically developed building systems, as did the French steel skeleton constructions for bridges, halls and towers. Wachsmann discovers a system applicable to all kinds of spatial load-bearing structures early on in Bell's tetrahedron, the most simple and stable spatial unit. From here he claims a genealogy of the principle of lightweight construction, which gained relevance under the influence of aviation, transport and the military.

The historic forays through the history of structural design read like an overture to the actual subject of the book: the exposition of the universal connector made from metal, invented and patented by Wachsmann. This was first used in the General Panel System, a prefabricated house system developed by Wachsmann and Walter Gropius in exile in the U.S. in 1941. The connector radically simplifies the construction process and simultaneously permits a wide range of combination options.

Gropius and Wachsmann shared an interest in the standardisation of housing construction. With the support of the State Research Society for Efficiency in Building and Housing (RFG), from 1926 to 1928 Walter Gropius was able to put the principles of prefabrication to the test in the Dessau-Törten housing development. Following its completion Gropius was subject to ongoing hostilities from local politicians who criticized the poor quality, construction and cultural expression of the buildings. The fierce attacks, which were also often personal in nature, may have given impetus to his decision to relocate to Berlin. Wachsmann worked from 1926 as an architect for the company Christoph & Unmack, which produced prefabricated timber frame houses. In 1931 he published the book *Holzhausbau: Technik und Gestaltung* (later published in English as *Building the Wooden House: Technique and Design*) about the experiences he had gathered there. After all, the company Döcker's wooden prisoners' barracks had made Christoph & Unmack wealthy during the First World War. In a refugee camp while fleeing Nazi Germany via France and Spain to New York, Wachsmann committed to paper his ideas on a new housing construction system. Gropius, who from 1937 was Professor of Architecture at Harvard University, had along with his German colleague Martin Wagner contributed to the American debates on the "defense housing problem". Wagner too was an architect of prefabrication; he also patented his MW House, a prefabricated and transportable round house, in 1942.

In the context of the U.S. war economy there was a fast-growing demand for housing for workers in the defence industry, which was to be combated with public housing programmes. Wachsmann and Gropius saw an opportunity here to actualize a construction kit for prefabricated houses. Reduced to a few panelling units and connecting elements, this system could be assembled not only by unskilled workers in just a few easy steps, but also in any location. Wachsmann pursued the aim of creating a universal building system in which the function of the individual elements always had to be designed into the generally accepted modular standard.[2] In this respect these were location-independent structures that could be used more or less anywhere in the world. As a result, the houses could now be completely industrially manufactured. It is therefore no coincidence that the plans, manufacturing systems and fabrication processes of Konrad Wachsmann's General Panel Corporation take equal place in the book: not the building site, but the factory, becomes the "epistemic location" where buildings are made.[3] The end of the war and the economic boom in the USA also transformed the housing market. The wartime experiences of standardized housing construction as flexible emergency accommodation now found a place in the mass production of the home as a consumer good. But in the context of the looming Cold War, for the "house-hungry nation" who wanted standardized prefabricated suburban developments as part of the American lifestyle promoted in media and magazines, the houses built using the perfected constructive General Panel System no longer offered the necessary cultural capital. In architectural history, the failure of this experiment in consistent industrial prefabrication has caused controversy. Reyner Banham spoke of one of the saddest episodes in the history of prefabrication: "it […] might have been a minor incident in the history of prefabrication, but it was a complete disaster within modern architecture, since it marked the failure of one of the most cherished dreams of Modernism."[4]

Wachsmann was possibly less interested in the economic success of this project than in what he had learned from the system's application. He continued to pursue the perfection of this systemic construction in both his teaching and his architectonic research projects: from the connector that bundled the information of the building system to the architecture of information in the punchcard.

Konrad Wachsmann, himself an immigrant, combined his interest in the rationalisation and standardisation of architecture with notions of universal applicability in different contexts: this claim to a "placeless architecture" is nonetheless infused with deep-seated ambiguities. Ultimately, the prefabrication and rationalisation of construction was closely intertwined with the war economy and colonialism and shaped their DNA. At the same time, this architecture of systems that Wachsmann had in common with some of his contemporaries also attempted to express in built form the knowledge culture of cybernetics and the atomic age.

In spite of the optimism towards technical development which accompanies these projects, even the critical architects' movements of the 1960s were inspired by these visions. Constant Nieuwenhuys, Cedric Price and Superstudio designed similar, flexible and open structures that countered the commercialised, zoned, alienated and capitalized built environment with spaces of imagination, potentiality and creativity. Despite diverse approaches and positions they were united by the conviction that universal combination options and maximum flexibility enabled everyone to become the designer of their own environment.

Konrad Wachsmann's universal connector, devised under the shadow cast by the Second World War and emigration and first used in 1941 in the General Panel System designed together with Walter Gropius, provided the starting point for the research of the Bauhaus Lab 2018.

1 Konrad Wachsmann, *The Turning Point of Building,* Van Nostrand Reinhold, New York, 1961.
2 Cf. Ibid.
3 Sascha Roesler, *Weltkonstruktionen,* Gebr. Mann Verlag, Berlin, 2013, 186.
4 Reyner Banham, 'I complessi della prefabbricazione', in: *Casabella*, Sept., vol. 50, no. 527, 1986, 29.

The postgraduate programme was part of the annual theme of the Bauhaus Dessau Foundation, *Standard*. After all, typing, norms and standardization were key to shaping an industrial culture at the Bauhaus.

Over three months, eight young international designers, curators and architectural historians conducted research into the metal universal connector, an object designed in the context of the war economy, emigration and experience of exile, which combines the ambiguities of the project of universal modern design in exemplary fashion. By considering the universal connector as an object/agent, the programme revealed the complex field of networks, environments, geographies, agents, institutions and materials in which this object operated. Through the lens of this thing *(Gegenstand)*, the participants explored how ideas and agendas of architectural research and building cultures materialised in these objects. The resulting collective exhibition in the Bauhaus Building took the modular raster of the General Panel System as the basis for an open structure that connected the diverse insights gained during the interdisciplinary research process in multiple ways.

Regina Bittner

The architect Konrad Wachsmann arrived in the U.S. in
1941, at the age of forty, a Jewish refugee fleeing the war
alongside one thousand other passengers crowded onto the
S.S. Navemar. When Wachsmann (1901–1980) entered the
port of New York on the morning of September 12, 1941,
he carries with him two sets of drawings he made while in
France. The drawings describe a new paradigm of building
using factory made parts that are joined together by inge-
nious connectors. The projects are a new architectural concept in which any conceivable type of building can be produced from these parts: a universal system of construction.

The project for a universal connector is the focal point of the
research undertaken by the Bauhaus Lab in 2018. Focusing
on the connectors has opened new links between the ideas
and projects of this architect and the complex dynamics of
colonialism, industrialization, consumerism, educational re-
forms, and conflict that unfolded throughout the 20th century.

The research traces the genealogy of architectural thinking
between the promises of technological and scientific progress and the stark effects of mechanization and war. From
the prefabricated houses produced during the Weimar Republic in the factory of Christoph & Unmack in Niesky, to the
American postwar homes of the General Panel Corporation,
"The Art of Joining" reflects the broad range of Wachsmann's
experiments on notions of "the standard," including his designs for innovative housing systems, automatic industrial
production lines, and experimental education schemes.

Wedge

The wedge connector is the universal joint at the heart of the General Panel Packaged House system designed by Konrad Wachsmann and Walter Gropius during Second World War. It is a standard joint that produces every necessary connection between building components. The system is developed in response to the need for rapid-built housing for defense workers in the wartime U.S.

The wedge connector radically simplifies the process of construction, enabling non-professionals to assemble a complete building. After the war ends, the need for mobility becomes irrelevant, and the system is retooled for permanent construction. New patents filed by General Panel Corporation in 1945 envision the wedge connector for civilian housing. Joining panels to build a suburban home, the connector plays a part in the growing area of home ownership.

The wedge connector's movement through different times and sites sets an alternative model for architecture, in which systems can create buildings for any use. But this also introduces a new role for the architect. They are no longer creators of individual buildings, but rather systems architects who define the means by which society builds.

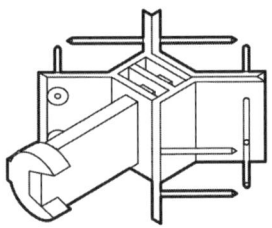

● Wedge Connector as brought to the U.S.
by Konrad Wachsmann.

THE WEDGE CONNECTOR: FROM FUNCTION TO SYMBOL

ELIZABETH ANDRZEJEWSKI

The wedge connector, a physical manifestation of Konrad Wachsmann's obsession with the *universal joint,* lies at the center of the development of the Packaged House System for the General Panel Corporation. The 1943 drawing set for the T.D.U.-1 version describes this system: "All the panel units are tightly connected with each other by a 'wedge connector' without using any nails, screws, hooks or glue for the assembly. The erection can be done by unskilled laborers who simply have to hammer in the tightening wedges… the small number of component parts of this system can be applied for an infinite variety of building types and building designs."[1] The design and development of the wedge connector actualizes theoretical concepts of open building systems, but, once the function of wedge connector evolved beyond its place within a panel, it became a symbol of the universal.

1 Konrad Wachsmann & Walter Gropius "Sectionalized Construction for Temporary Dwelling Units, National Housing Agency, Federal Public Housing Authority, Type T.D.U.-1.", General Panel Corporation, New York City, NY, 1943, Harvard Art Museums, Somerville Research Facility.

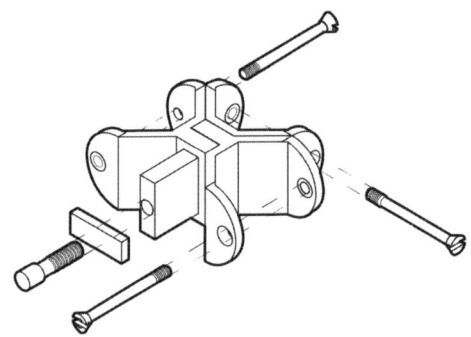

● Wachsmann and Gropius begin working together.

The wedge connector underwent three distinct periods of transformation between 1939–47, culminating in the release of Wachsmann's book *The Turning Point of Building* in 1959. The first design phase included a Y-shaped design complicated by fastening nails and screws as well as a prescribed assembly order.

Then the wedge connector was flattened and simplified between 1942 and 1945 to provide the mobility, speed, and efficiency required by the U.S. government during Second World War. Finally, the third evolution of the wedge connector, today the best known version, features a four-part demountable design.

In 1941 Wachsmann emigrated from France to the U.S. carrying initial plans for the Y-shaped wedge connector, which together with infill wall panels, made up a concept for a panelized universal building system. Following the U.S. entry into Second World War after the attack on Pearl Harbor on December 7, 1941, Konrad Wachsmann and Walter Gropius adapt the wedge connector to the U.S. standard system of measurement and further simplify the design in Boston. These initial designs for the Y-shaped wedge connector relied on nails and other fastening devices which made the concept cumbersome. However, they set the groundwork for the universal concept. Second World War was a design catalyst and an opportunity for both the wedge connector and the fledgling General Panel Corporation.

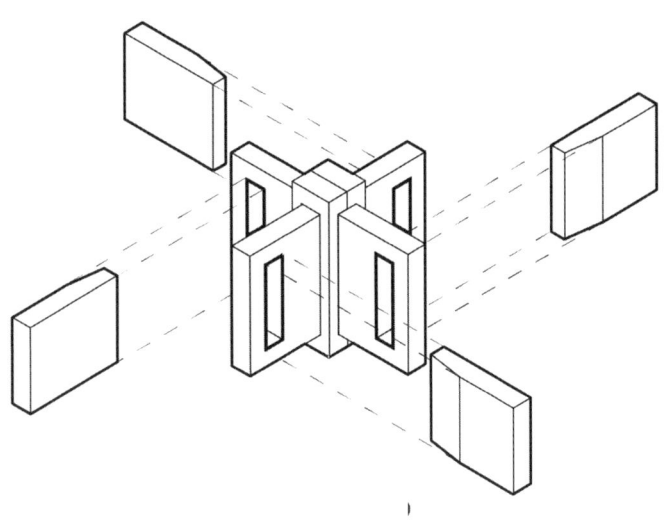

● Wedge Connector as brought to the U.S.
by Konrad Wachsmann.

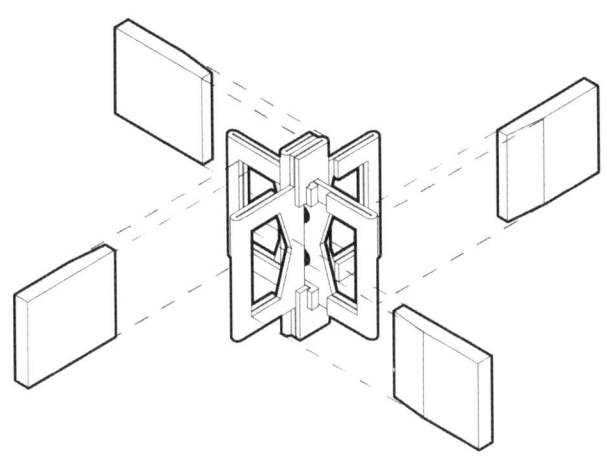

● Sectionalized Construction for Temporary
Dwelling Units, Type T.D.U.-1.

When the Federal Works Agency allocated $153 million for demountable housing for defense workers in February of 1942, the Packaged House System seemed to offer a prefabricated, temporary housing solution to the problem identified by the government.[2] The wedge connector described in the patent for "Prefabricated Building", U.S. 2,355,192, was further simplified into two-dimensional pieces that slid together to make it more suitable for quick, efficient, and mobile wartime housing. In 1943 the wedge connector evolved further still as the system was adapted to meet the requirements of the U.S. Government for the temporary defense housing program. This folded version of the wedge connector reduced overall material weight during the wartime metal shortage. It was demonstrated to the U.S. Plywood Corporation, military officials, public housing authorities, and government representatives in Somerville, Massachusetts in 1943.

2   Gilbert Herbert, *The Dream of the Factory-Made House: Walter Gropius and Konrad Wachsmann*, The MIT Press, Cambridge, 1986.

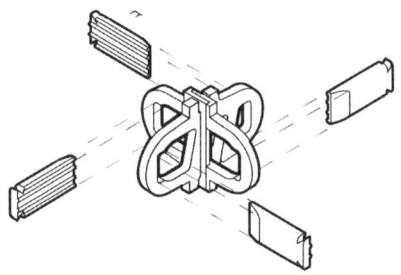

● U.S. Patent 2,421,305 "Building Structure."

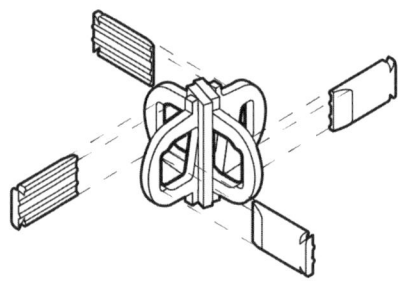

● Factory production of the wedge continues until 1951.

As Second World War ended, the wedge connector evolved once more to suit the needs of a new market for private homes. The patent filed in 1945, "Building Structure," U.S. 2,421,305, depicts a version of the wedge connector consisting of four metal pieces and four wedges for slotting into panels. This patent describes how the wedge connector was changed to make it more suitable for permanent housing. This version eliminated the closure strips of the past, which had facilitated demountability, in favor of the ideal aesthetics of smooth walls. Contracts for the Packaged House System and Government housing programs fueled the design of a factory, which was completed in 1947. At the factory, the wedge connector was inserted into panels mechanically, and then fixed between layers of finish material. The wedge connector's universal qualities were diminished in favor of a speedy prefabricated assembly system, contradicting the original intentions for demountability and flexibility.

Divorced from its fixed function within a panel, the wedge connector rests as a symbol of the universal joint. Wachsmann's initial attempts to manifest the concept of universality into a physical form through the Packaged House System failed to be realized. However, the abstract principles of universal building, derived from this full-scale development, are lasting. Universal building can be achieved through the design of open systems that are free from scale, limitations of workforce, site, and material specificity. These four principles were first symbolized in a four-part universal joint: the wedge connector.

House

To mitigate the damage created by the Great Depression and Second World War, the United States government developed a progressive economic policy, lending money to the construction and finance sectors, so that they would build and offer veterans and young families the opportunity to obtain low-cost mortgages to purchase homes. Before the 1940s, most families in the U.S. did not own their home. A new wave of private home ownership would create a cultural phenomenon.

During the war years, public institutions and publications introduced the idea of "New American Housing for the New Worker" through articles and exhibitions. It was believed that the U.S. public would begin to accept mass-produced housing and modern architectural styles due to the mechanization in manufacturing they had become accustomed to during the war.

● Richard Neutra, House design for General Panel System, 1944.

YOUR (GENERAL PANEL) HOME
RHIANNON HAYCOCK

In 1943 and 1944, the magazine *Arts & Architecture* held two house design competitions, the first to design a house for "Post-War Living," and the second sponsored by U.S. Plywood Association. The winning designs appeared to appeal to the general public when they were exhibited. During this time, Walter Gropius assigned his students at Harvard with the task of designing houses using the Packaged House System, and the well-known architects Richard Neutra, Paul Bromberg and Ferdinand Kramer produced watercolor renderings of housing designs for General Panel Corporation. The designs were to highlight "the greatest possible standardization with the greatest possible variation in form."[1] This they achieved: the houses varied in style and visual impact, but reflected the "International Modern" type.

In 1946, General Panel Corp won a contract from the veteran housing program to create 10,000 units of their Packaged House System. By the time the company was ready to start production this program had been revoked. General Panel Corp then entered the low-cost individual housing market. The houses designed by famous architects were not featured in the "Your General Panel Home" brochure released in 1946. The house in the brochure is a four-room single story building, the typical entry-level house for many mass-production housing companies of the time. Typologically it stands alone.

---

1 "Walter Gropius and the not so infinite possibilities of prefabrication." *AIAAC* 4th Quarter, 2007.

The standardized Packaged House system, with its ten different panel types to be configured in several combinations, always creates a building with a hint of the "International Modern" style. At this time, the most popular low-cost house in United States was named the "Cape Cod," a New England style cottage. The building was constructed of the same materials as the General Panel house, but the historical design of its exterior is recognizably North American, giving the consumer in this emerging economy the ability to buy a sense of rootedness to place after the uncertainties of war.

The General Panel House was not the only low-cost building to diverge from the vernacular in its design: Lustron Houses were constructed of steel and porcelain in a former munitions plant, and they departed from the traditional aesthetic of General Panel's competitors. However, their marketing material uses color illustrations and photographs of family life, such as a woman sat at a vanity table or a child on his bed playing, featured alongside diagrams showing how the latest technology in the home creates a comfortable living environment. The advertisements are reminiscent of the illustrations in catalogues for houses from the 19th and early 20th century, thus creating a sense of nostalgia. Some mass developers, such as Levitt and Sons, didn't use interior images in their brochures. Rather they created textual narratives describing the suburbs they were creating, enabling the consumer to visualize their new home. By comparison, the General Panel brochure appears functional, the photographs of the interior of the house are staged with the latest kitchen equipment, and furniture by Eames and other

YOUR GENERAL PANEL HOME...

designed for

Comfortable Living

Your General Panel Home offers solid comfort, modern beauty, convenient livability. Here is a home far advanced in design and so carefully styled that it is a perfect setting for the furniture mode of your taste. . . . from Chinese Modern to Traditional. There are no unnecessary proportions or cut up wall areas to rob you of usable space –then, you can arrange and rearrange your furnishings to suit your fancy.

And for your pleasure and enjoyment the walls will be finished in either high grade paint or wallpaper to your choice of colors.

The living room, with its wall of floor-to-ceiling full-length picture windows, overlooks your veranda and front garden, giving you a feeling of spaciousness by "bringing the outdoors in," and accenting airiness with plenty of light and proper ventilation.

Yes, this, your living room, typifies the care and consideration that have gone into every phase of designing and building your General Panel Home.

3

● *General Panel System Catalogue*, 1946.

designers created circa 1946, but is devoid of any ephemera, art or people. Where the Lustron advertisements show how technology can enable comfortable living, the *General Panel* brochure devotes as many pages to architectural technology and the efficiency of assemblage. Wachsmann's "Erection Manual," with a sequence of tasks so detailed that the house could be built without traditional instructions, may have been of interest to an architect, a building enthusiast or the corporate buyer, but it is not selling the American dream to the aspiring middle classes.

The purchaser of a General Panel house would take on the role of contractor, surveyor and estate agent: they would have to find a plot of land to build their home on, and undertake the work to link the new house to local utilities. Many of the most successful mass house builders of the time, whether selling prefabricated houses or not, would offer a plot of land and the management of linking to services, whilst others such as Levitt and Sons, and Sears Roebuck & Co went further and developed "towns" in the suburbs, with pools, schools and shopping malls. They created a community to join, all within commutable distance to the city.

A sense of community was integral to the development of a postwar society. In Europe this had developed into socialist policies being implemented in many of the former Allied countries. To stop this ideology from growing in popularity, the U.S. government encouraged the promotion of individual wealth and home ownership as the "American Dream" available to all. Low cost, factory-built houses were

- *Thousand Lanes.* Spring – Summer 1959.

● *General Panel System Catalogue,* 1946.

promoted as the ideal site to become part of a community and to express your individuality, through the consumption of products for your home and your life. Many of the pre-fabricated housing producers partnered with department stores and magazines to advertise products and publish articles on how to customize your factory-built home. The Package House system had featured in several industry specific journals, including *Architectural Forum,* and Gropius is thought to have promoted it as a social housing solution overseas, but there isn't evidence of promotion to the U.S. mass market of low-cost home buyers through the mainstream publications.

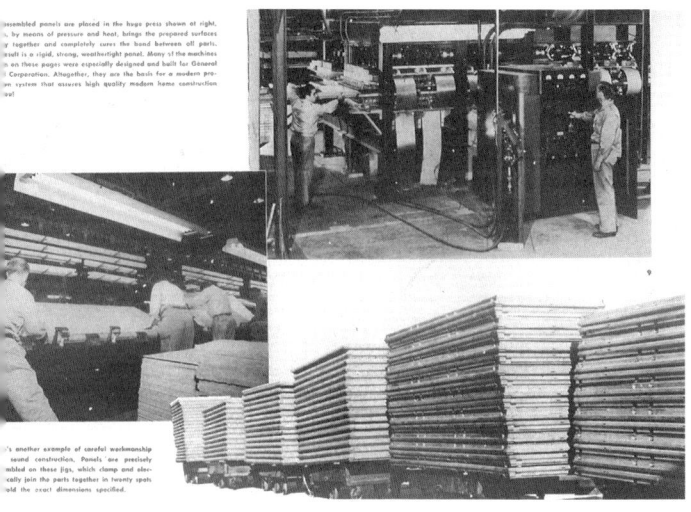

In the immediate postwar years, the most popular low-cost houses were traditional, American-style houses that city-dwelling Americans once admired, and could now buy to be their home in a suburban development. Although these houses were traditional on the outside, the lives they framed were increasingly modern. In the late 1940s there was an open dialog in the media about what the American home-owner wanted; a home that was mechanized and fit for their community[2].

2 "A Roundtable on Housing" *Life* Magazine, January 1949, 73-86.

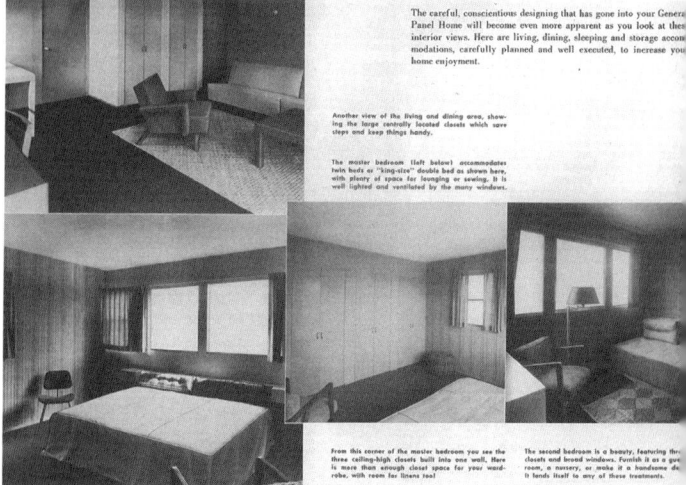

The careful, conscientious designing that has gone into your General Panel Home will become even more apparent as you look at these interior views. Here are living, dining, sleeping and storage accommodations, carefully planned and well executed, to increase your home enjoyment.

Another view of the living and dining area, showing the large centrally located closets which save steps and keep things handy.

The master bedroom (left below) accommodates twin beds or "king-size" double bed as shown here, with plenty of space for lounging or sewing. It is well lighted and ventilated by the many windows.

From this corner of the master bedroom you see the three ceiling-high closets built into one wall. Here is more than enough closet space for your wardrobe, with room for linens too!

The second bedroom is a beauty, featuring three closets and broad windows. Furnish it as a guest room, a nursery, or make it a handsome den. It lends itself to any of these treatments.

● *General Panel System Catalogue,* 1946.

Consumers were becoming decidedly knowledgeable about design technology and increasingly wanted more sophisticated products to furnish their homes, so it was inevitable that the desire for modern design would permeate into architecture. The Packaged House system does not feature in this discourse, the architect-designed modern house that framed furniture that would become 20th century design classics had missed its time, just as the new "American Modern" was capturing the imagination of consumers, General Panel was failing. Wachsmann's increasing obsession with perfecting the systems of construction meant costs would spiral out of control, and the company closed in 1951. It is believed that only 200 Packaged Houses were ever produced.

dining area, handily located near
kitchen, is set off from the rest of
living area. Again you find that
magic of large windows means
at you may enjoy meals in the com-
rt of indoors, but with that out-of-
ors charm that is a part of West-
living.

One of the most important features of your
General Panel Home is that it comes to you
complete, ready for you to move into, with
no hidden costs to increase your home
investment. Moreover, you will easily see
that — compared to today's conventional
construction — your General Panel Home
gives you more for your money . . . more
quality . . . more lasting beauty . . . pre-
cision workmanship.

ecial features of the bathroom are: cove-
ased linoleum floors with easy-to-clean
unded corners; splash-proof, easy-to-wash
eet plastic wainscoting around the entire
om; high-quality chromium fixtures.

The moment you step into this kitchen you're amazed
at its well-planned, step-saving efficiency. Compact,
yes—but large enough for several "helpers" without
crowding. Gleaming white cabinets and sink . .
cupboard space galore . . . and plenty of working
space. There's proper light and ventilation the year
'round, supplied by the broad windows which in
addition to being so practical will make a pleasant
frame for your garden view. Efficiency, utility and
beauty combine to make this a kitchen in which you
will enjoy working.

5

Niesky: In an unpublished biography written late in his life, Konrad Wachsmann reflected on the origins of his practice: "Everything that followed, everything that came about in Berlin, New York, Tokyo, Chicago, London, Moscow, Paris, Rome, Zurich, Warsaw — all that, surprisingly enough, had its beginnings in Niesky, a narrow, provincial village. In this wooden construction company I discovered the way that led me to the turning point in building…" The young and ambitious architect left the metropolis of Berlin in 1926. He traveled to a small village situated in the middle of Saxony's forest. This particular destination was recommended to him by his professor Hans Poelzig. It was through Poelzig that Wachsmann was given a three-year contract as full-time architect in the industrial enterprise of a Danish carpenter Christian Ferdinand Christoph and architect Christian Rudolf Unmack. At first, Christoph & Unmack AG must have appeared to the architect as peripheral. It was geographically alienated from any intellectual circles of Weimar Republic. However, as the above recollection suggests, it was Niesky that became a place of "turning point in building" for the architect. The future and revolution in architecture was not to originate at the university, experimental school or in an architectural office. For Wachsmann it was based in the factory production line, like the one that he encountered in Christoph & Unmack — the biggest and oldest production of prefabricated timber buildings in Europe of the 1920s.

Wachsmann's early professional experience can be seen as a key to understanding his later career and life. In Europe this was the experience of an author, of "Building The Wooden House — Technique and Design," published in 1931; after crossing the Atlantic, when he was granted an intellectual refugee status, of a renowned expert of wooden structures; and finally in the U.S., where he started to work on the systems later patented by the General Panel Corporation. At the same time, as I would like to argue, looking at Wachsmann's early career can reveal a different set of histories. These are histories of industrialized housing production which entangle a modern architectural development with the global scope of colonial frontiers between 19th and 20th century. Simultaneously, they constitute the basis for a better understanding of Wachsmann's practice and designs both during the Second World War and in the postwar period.

Christoph & Unmack: At the point of Wachsmann's arrival in Niesky, the market success and global reach of the timber houses produced in the factory of Christoph & Unmack had been ongoing for decades. A closer look at this process points to a particular set of patents acquired in 1882 in Copenhagen by Christian Ferdinand Christoph and Christian Rudolf Unmack from Captain of Royal Danish Army, Johan Gerhard Clemens Döcker. Döcker's patents described and illustrated a new system of construction in a technical manner: "The object of this invention is to provide a structure for use either in the military service or for other purposes of such a construction and material as to be light, durable, readily set up or taken down again and adapted to be packed in a com-

Joh. Gerh. Clemens Doecker

Chr. F. Christoph

Chr. Rud. Unmack

Älteste Barackenform

Neuester Pavillonbau

−1882−   −1907−

● "Family tree" of Döcker buildings, in: *Ein Vierteljahrhundert im Dienste der Gesundheitspflege und Volkswohlfahrt in Krieg und Frieden,* commemorative publication of barrack factory, Christoph & Unmack AG, 1907.

● Holzbauten in alle Länder, Company Prospect,
Christoph & Unmack AG Niesky/OL, Niesky, 1938.

paratively limited space in a closed box." It was therefore nothing else but a system of barrack construction, enabling the production of simple, durable, cheap, and most importantly mobile architectural structures. The purchase of patents was quickly followed by a success of Döcker barracks produced by the company resulting in prizes at the 1883 Berlin Hygiene Exhibition (*Berliner Hygiene-Ausstellung*) and Antwerp Barracks Competition of 1885 (*Antwerpener Baracken-Wettbewerb*). New, larger commissions arrived as well, mainly from the Prussian army in need of hospital and military buildings which could be used domestically and abroad.

Production was moved to Niesky. The choice of the place was far from accidental. Dense local forests provided an abundance of crucial raw material. However, much more importantly it was in Niesky that Christian Ferdinand's uncle, Johannes Ehregott Christoph, was running a major steel industrial plant. The village was therefore geographically distant from big urban centers but infrastructurally connected to the global market. Finally, Niesky and its surroundings were populated with followers of a Moravian Church, including Christoph's uncle, who settled there after centuries of persecution and escaped from the territories of modern day Czechia. A crucial part of the church's activity was its missionary practice. The standardized and prefabricated mobile buildings, among which were both simple barracks and elaborated churches, soon became a part of the equipment of missionaries traveling to countries spread around the global south.

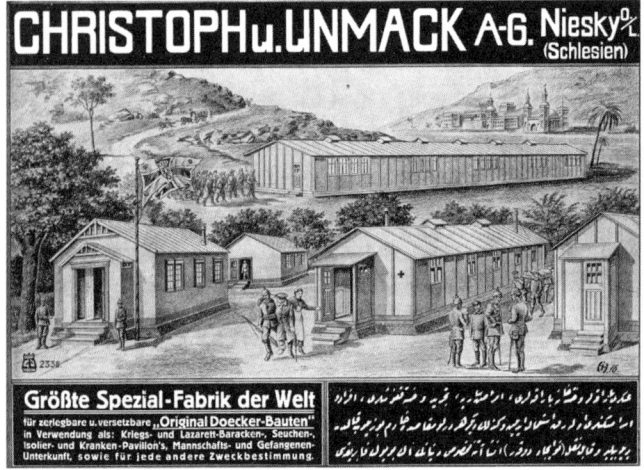

● Advertisement for Döcker buildings, newspaper clipping, before 1918.

Meanwhile, Christoph & Unmack production in Niesky was growing year after year chiefly through the orders for military and hospital barracks: in 1892 the packaged structures were sent to Hamburg to support the fight against the cholera epidemic; in 1900 they traveled to China with an international military coalition sent there from Europe during the Boxer Uprising; in 1904, barracks provided infrastructure for the Russian army during its war with Japan; finally, in 1905, barracks traveled with the army and colonists to German South West Africa.[1]

1 Heinrich Wurm, "Die Industrialisierung des Holzhausbaues: Christoph und Unmack", *Tradition: Zeitschrift für Firmengeschichte und Unternehmerbiographie 14,* No. 3/4, 1969, 198-211.

In the latter instance, we can observe how a mobile, durable and standardized prefabricated building became a direct answer to spatial challenges of the frontier capitalist economy at the peak moment of colonial era. Decrees signed in Berlin in 1884 between the European colonizers inaugurated the process of the so-called "Scramble for Africa." Imperial influence on the African continent moved towards full military subordination and extraction of labor and resources. This process took place on the frontiers of capitalism which through their social and climatic conditions presented an array of disadvantages to European colonizers. The prefabricated Döcker barrack was an infrastructural remedy, easing that process.

While the surge in the Döcker barrack production lasted, Christoph & Unmack developed by turning towards other architectural uses for standardized timber buildings. The possibilities were enormous, spanning across all possible utilitarian functions: from those related to hygiene, through temporary entertainment pavilions, sport facilities and schools, to individual family houses of different forms and styles. During the years leading up to First World War, hundreds of those buildings were advertized in catalogs and newspapers, presented at housing exhibitions across Prussia, erected in Niesky and beyond. During the time in which professional architects of the modern movement in Germany such as Walter Gropius only started to discuss the idea of industrially produced dwellings, Christoph & Unmack was applying a variety of patented timber prefabrication systems of varied complexity and use. In this process, a traditional labor-intensive and localized practice of building was transformed into a highly rationalized, calculable and industrially organized production process: a change characteristic for every useful object which underwent a process of commodification within the 19th century industrial capitalism.

Weimar Republic: During First World War, Christoph & Unmack grew exponentially, employing 4,000 workers, focusing exclusively on supplementing infrastructures for the Prussian War Ministry. However, the heyday of state-funded military construction finishes in 1918, as the country loses the war and is stripped of its colonies by the League of Nations, and descends into the era of financial turmoil in the 1920s. The company's core product, the barracks, suddenly became obsolete, or this is how it seemed. In 1921 the timber construction factory merges with industrial plant of Christoph's uncle. The conglomerate starts to develop a new offer which, on the one hand, focuses on train carriages, and, on the other, moves towards production of houses for individual use. This specialization is further stimulated by the housing crisis which overshadows the whole period. The flexibility of the construction systems allows for a smooth transition from military use to a wide variety of utilitarian to commercially attractive applications, aiming to compete on the domestic and world markets.

In the 1920s Christoph & Unmack starts to consult its home designs with respected architects such as Hans Poelzig and Hans Scharoun, presenting its timber houses along prominent designs during exhibitions, such as at the Berlin Werk-

● Test construction of a prefabricated log cabin in Christoph & Unmack workshop, in: *Holzbau-Industriellen-Verband, Deutscher Holzhausbau – Eine Monographie des deutschen Holzhausbaus,* Berlin, 1921.

bund Exhibition in 1924. It also maintains the production designs reaching the frontiers of the colonized world. The offer of Christoph & Unmack houses is advertised in the catalogs distributed widely by post. The improvement of graphic design of such catalogs becomes Wachsmann's task while he stays in Niesky. Several catalogs from that time remain in the archive, notably one with a particularly global span. *Export Catalogue of Wooden Buildings* was published in 1926 in four languages reaching the whole colonial world—German, English, French and Spanish. It presents several types of buildings predominantly designed in the Döcker system. Simple barracks are used here as a basis for more sophisticated colonial huts, which responded both to the climate conditions of the global south and the aesthetic tastes of colonizers regarding the architecture and interiors. Different variants of "Movable Houses for Tropics" are represented through images of houses with white colonists and their indigenous servants of a darker skin color. Houses feature elevated floor and roof openings, which were meant to achieve a better circulation of air and, as it was believed, create a more hygienic environment. In all the designs the typical feature of colonial housing is present—veranda—the architectural concept which was introduced in German language only during that period.[2] Houses are presented in the export catalog along the crucial utilitarian functions of prefabricated structures—hospitals, schools, chapels and prayer houses.

2   Itohan Osayimwese, *Colonialism and Modern Architecture in Germany,* University of Pittsburgh Press, Pittsburgh, 2017, 9.

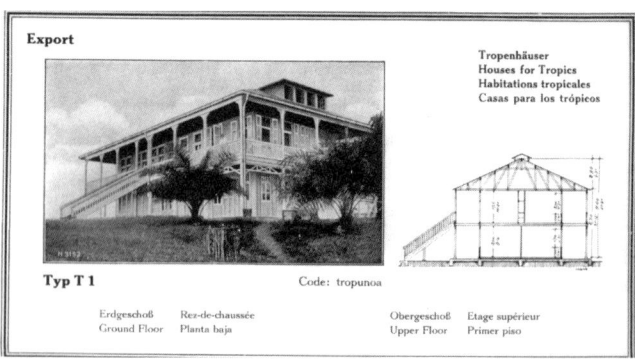

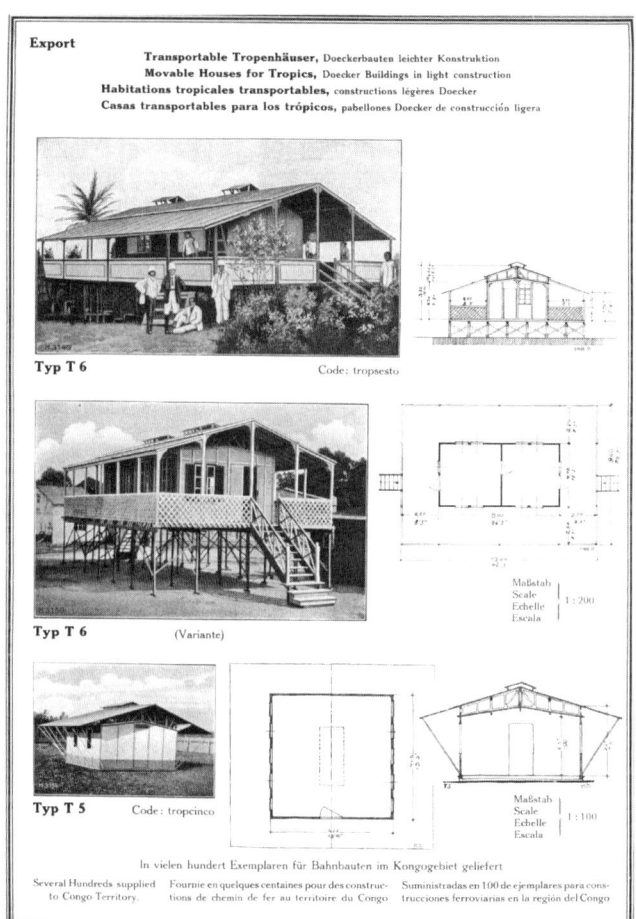

- Movable Houses for Tropics, *Export Catalogue of Wooden Buildings.* Christoph & Unmack AG Niesky/OL, 1926.

The export catalog finishes with a set of permanent houses based on the "Boarded Frame system" which points towards other construction systems employed in the late 1920s by Christoph & Unmack. All of them form the technical basis for Wachsmann's 1931 book *Building The Wooden House — Technique and Design.* It is a publication addressed to a broader public, which, as the architect suggests, is meant to change the negative opinion of timber construction. The book presents three main systems of prefabricated timber construction, all of which were employed in Christoph & Unmack construction — log method, boarded frame method and panel method. The invention of the last one Wachsmann assigns to himself. "The Panel Method" can therefore be considered as a predecessor of housing prefabrication systems developed by the architect in the 1940s under the General Panel Corporation. Construction using the panel method is described by Wachsmann as the most standardized system, which allows for the extensive prefabrication in the factory halls and delivery to the most remote sites. The process of construction is illustrated with a series of horizontal photos inserted between lines of the text. The photo descriptions indicates a 1929 construction of a large hotel for Curaçao, at the time a Dutch colony near the coast of Venezuela. The design is one of the very few which Wachsmann signed himself as a designer on behalf of Christoph & Unmack. Archival documents indicate that the hotel was built for an unnamed oil company. Since the early colonial era Curaçao became a transitional port between Europe and both Americas. Its importance surged after Anglo-Dutch Royal Dutch Shell discovered rich sources of oil in Venezuela's Lake Maracaibo near Curaçao in 1910. The Royal Dutch Shell established an oil refinery on the island and set infrastructure for larger transport vessels to dock at its coast. This infrastructure was expanded in 1927 and, as a result, the workforce of the company on the island increased to almost 11,000 people in 1929. It was therefore the Royal Dutch Company who ordered Christoph & Unmack, with Konrad Wachsmann as its architect, to provide a prefabricated hotel for an island located thousands of kilometers from Niesky. The most standardized and technologically advanced method of prefabrication was employed to smoothly facilitate a process of expansion of the growing colonial exploitation of natural resources of Venezuela. Here, yet again we observe, how the developments in production, flexibility and mobility of architecture arose as a response to the frontier character of capitalist exploitation and extraction of value.

"Standardization Takes Command": Konrad Wachsmann was part of a generation which allowed him to work and contribute to the modern movement in its interwar "heroic period," of wartime transition and the postwar era. His work, while influential in the sphere of education, theory, speculation and experimental design, remained unrealized on a larger scale. Tracing the origins of Wachsmann's thinking about standardization and industrialization to his employment in Christoph & Unmack AG, we were able to substantially extend the scope of our inquiry. Barracks, because of their simplicity and industrial origin, scarcely constitute a subject for traditional architectural histories dealing with transformation, development and improvements of building forms by recognized figures in the architectural field. However, a broad proliferation of this typology and its presence across the world proves to be a source of histories which reframe the scope of architectural production in modernity.

From Konrad Wachsmann through Walter Gropius to Le Corbusier, the discussions on prefabrication re-emerged after the Second World War across the globe. In a few decades it materialized in concrete while applied in the state-driven housing constructions on both sides of the Iron Curtain. And while this part of prefabrication history is recognized and present in contemporary building, Wachsmann's early career points toward wood and barracks as material predecessors of concrete panels and housing projects. Simultaneously, histories of standard wooden houses in the early modern era underline how this commodified and mobile architecture became an extension of the capitalist market of the colonial era, facilitating the domination of European empires the frontiers of their expansion. Finally, while the modern movement is today a historical phenomenon, barracks remain a basic architectural typology offering mobile, standardized, industrially produced containers marking different frontiers and borders in the globally connected world — housing workers in the special economic zones in the global south, and migrants in the heart of Europe.

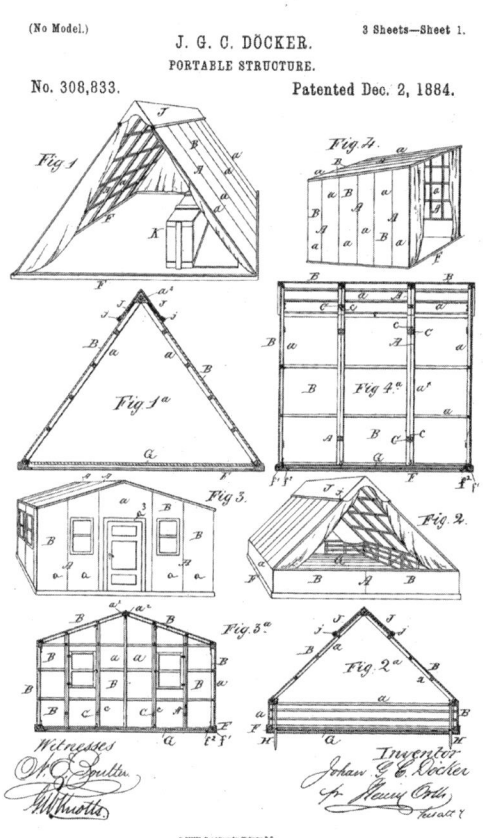

J. G. C. DÖCKER.

PORTABLE STRUCTURE.

No. 308,833.

Patented Dec. 2, 1884.

● Johan Gerhard Clemens Döcker, Portable Structure, U.S. Patent No. 308,833, issued December 2, 1884.

Epilog: The factory-made house produces visions of an ultimate universal system that can be applied to any housing or building need. This dream encapsulates a building as a product ready to roll off standardized assembly lines like cars. Many have tried to bring this vivid dream to fruition, as Konrad Wachsmann attempted in the 1940s. However, the ultimate reality of prefabrication is often much more complicated than producing all the parts necessary to assemble a house. Even today, prefabrication appears to offer a catch-all solution for housing shortage and crisis, such is the case with the IKEA Better Shelter, which aims to help house refugees. The dream always considers the following benefits in some respect: cost savings, better quality, ability to be erected anywhere, quick assembly by unskilled people, and ability to be reused or expanded. The "Better Shelter" exemplifies a contemporary prefabricated housing solution that makes promises similar to that of the General Panel Corporation. In the nature of IKEA, the shelter system is factory produced, flat-packed, and easily shipped. As a product, the Better Shelter promises "A Home Away from Home" that is safe and dignified, sustainable, cost efficient, modular, adaptable, and easy to assemble and disassemble. Teams of four refugees become the equivalents of General Panel's unskilled laborers, assembling their own identical home in about four hours, depending on experience level. Once erected directly on the ground, the house remains dynamic and can be added to or later demounted and moved along with the refugee.

Time and again, prefabrication has been hailed as a universal solution to efficient housing that provides better quality at lower cost. However, while the factory provides many benefits, such as the cost-effective production of parts, the outputs are often less than ideal. While General Panel did provide a system to produce housing, the transition from the standardized system to a customized home and lifestyle never took off. Similarly, while the Better Shelter is undoubtedly a substantially better alternative to living in a tent as part of life in a refugee camp, it still does not offer refugees a true home with basic amenities such as running water, sewage, and access to food. It resembles a better barrack—Elizabeth Andrzejeski

Factory

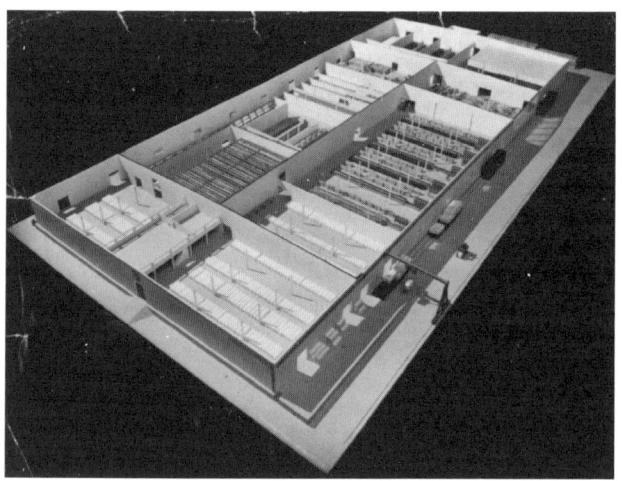

● General Panel Corporation factory, Burbank, California,
model. Photograph by Anna Wachsmann.

Planning for a General Panel production plant began in 1946, when the company purchased a disused Lockheed Aircraft Corporation engine factory in Burbank, California from the U.S. government. The design of the plant took a year to complete, with the production line planned to incorporate the most advanced, automatic industrial equipment available. When the factory was ready to start production in the summer of 1947, it had the capability of producing panels for as many as 10,000 houses per year.

Before the plant in California was completed, a scale model was produced and displayed in the General Panel offices in New York, where Konrad Wachsmann and Walter Gropius worked on the design of the company's products and facilities, and courted potential investors. The miniature factory functioned as a working model while Wachsmann perfected its layout, scripting the flow of materials through the building. But after this design work was finished, the model became a rhetorical tool.

General Panel, which was perpetually short on cash, needed to find new investors in order to raise funds for its factory. An initial round of investments from friends and acquaintances—including the famous architecture historian Sigfried Giedion—raised some capital for the development of the system, but other sources were needed to realize the model at full-scale, on-site. Three thousand miles away from the real factory, the model was the next best way to persuade visitors and would-be investors that the company knew what it was doing.

What can be said of Konrad Wachsmann's teaching? The architect's designs for prefabricated building systems are well-known, but his pedagogical career has been somewhat overlooked. This fact is curious if only because Wachsmann was ultimately a more prolific teacher than builder, and this parallel activity extended almost continuously from his appointment to the faculty of the "New Bauhaus" in Chicago, in 1950, until his death in Los Angeles in 1980. Indeed, Wachsmann's best-known architectural projects, such as the demountable hangar system for the U.S. Air Force, came about only by virtue of his academic work: the hangar was developed and executed with the help of a team of graduate students in the architect's research group in Chicago. In light of Wachsmann's passion for systematicity, it seems appropriate to ask the question directly: what is the pedagogy of systems?

If the aim of the architect's universal building systems was to provide a construction technique with universal applications, that is, systems appropriate to any use and outcome, then how could this ideal be taught in a manner that was similarly open-ended? Wachsmann's answer was, of course, systematic. Beginning in the 1950s, the architect developed a set of instructional techniques, a "teaching system," that enacted a strict protocol for classroom activity, but which conspicuously *did not* define content or curriculum. Every workshop would proceed thus: students, ideally 21 of them, work collaboratively on a design problem. The group divides the problem into seven sub-problems, which are then addressed by teams of three students each. The teams then share their findings with one another in a series of structured conversations and build up the solution collaboratively. These techniques were the script for the Salzburg Summer Academy workshops held in the 1950s, in which students (one year including the young Hans Hollein), worked collaboratively on a design project. The 1956 academy designed and constructed a chalet for Sigfried Giedion in Amden.

Wachsmann's last major project developed this systematic pedagogical format as the basis of a permanent research center in Los Angeles. This organization, known as the Building Institute at the University of California, represents a significantly more complex application of the teamwork concept, integrating purpose-built spaces, a unique organizational towards structure, and cybernetic principles of information control toward the production of research. The history of this organization demonstrates how the production of a pedagogical system was aligned with the project of resituating the architect as an agent working to affect larger systems and structures beyond the studio: university, industry, and as Wachsmann wrote in the Building Institute's founding documents, no less than "The Society of Man" itself. (See diagram on pages 142–143 in this volume.)

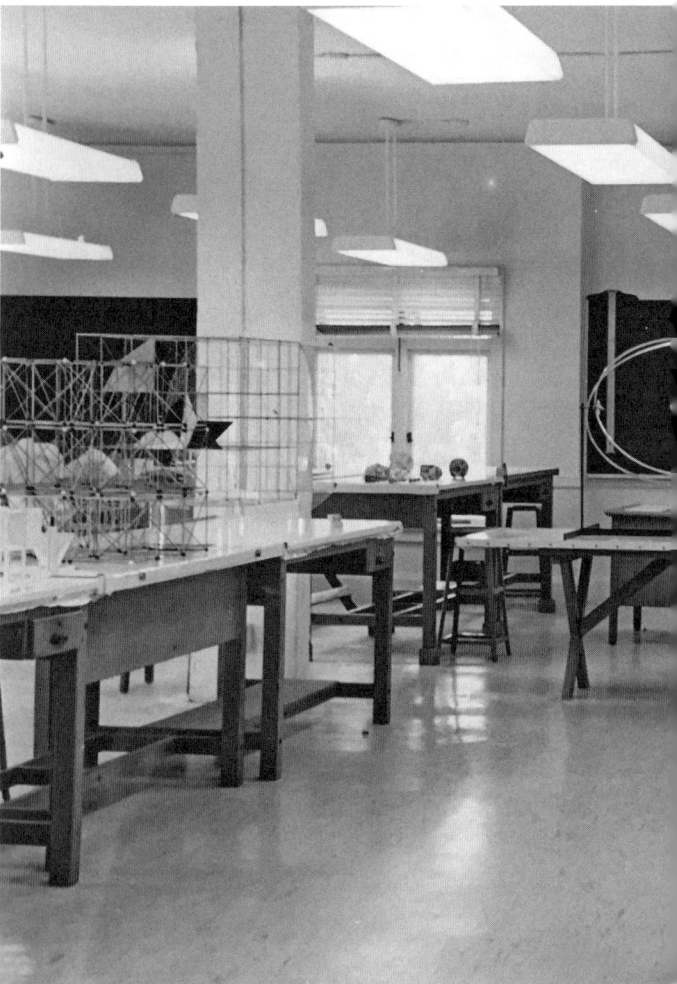

● Main work-
space at the
Building
Institute, circa
1970.

Planning for the Building Institute at USC began in Italy in 1963. Crombie Taylor, a former colleague of Wachsmann's at the Institute of Design in Chicago, had been appointed associate dean of the School of Architecture in Los Angeles. Working in Genoa on what would ultimately be an ill-fated project to redesign the city's port district, Wachsmann went to Los Angeles without hesitation. At USC, Taylor handed down a directive to reconceive the school's graduate programs, and accordingly, Wachsmann undertook a year-long study for the potential curriculum. This preliminary work was funded by the Graham Foundation, and took the form of a series of diagrams published in '64. Wachsmann's proposed answer was the Building Institute, a research center that would allow graduate students to work collaboratively on funded research under the direction of the faculty, in pursuit of the degree Master of Building Science.

In some ways, the Institute replicated a model for conducting sponsored research that Wachsmann had developed at the Institute of Design a decade earlier. In Chicago, a government contract to produce a prefabricated system for aircraft hangars had allowed Wachsmann and several students to develop tubular steel space frame structures over the course of five years. The Institute would also be premised on sponsored research, but finding sponsors was a problem at first. Although Wachsmann had been appointed in 1964, it wasn't until three years later, in 1967, that the Institute received its first sponsored research grant. In the meanwhile, the Institute pursued technical research in the context of Wachsmann's architecture practice, which was then engaged in the design of a city hall for California City. Although this project supported the Institute and its investigators, it represented just one small facet of the organization's stated mission as a "center of study, research, development, and information related to all aspects of industrialization and its impact upon planning and architecture."[1]

The founder of the Building Institute imagined that it would be the nucleus of a continuously expanding network of allied disciplines spanning the sciences and the arts. In a memo to the university president, Wachsmann outlined six basic components of the program: basic research, applied research, student training, teacher training, a doctoral program in building science, and an information center. The Institute would act as a medium for leveraging the combined expertise of the university towards the transformation of the built environment. The scope and shape of the organization's mission had been defined in the series of diagrams that Wachsmann drafted soon after arriving in California, but it was the design of the Institute's space that would be tasked with translating these concepts into physical space.

1 "Memo to Dr. Milton C. Kloetzel, Proposal to Authorize the Creation of a Building Institute, May 22, 1968", in: Crombie Taylor Papers, Ryerson and Burnham Libraries of the Art Institute of Chicago, Box 5, Series 19, Memos, Wachsmann USC.

● Buckminster Fuller and Konrad Wachsmann in conversation in front of an image of the California City project. Taken at the opening of the exhibition "Konrad Wachsmann: 50 Years of Life and Work Toward Industrialization of Building," at the USC Fisher Gallery in 1971.

As campus protests against the Vietnam War reached a boiling point at the end of the 1960s, Wachsmann, who had worked for the U.S. military during and after Second World War, established the Institute on the edge of the USC campus, in what was formerly the armory of the 160th Army Infantry Regiment. The building was well-suited to the Institute's needs: the vast drill hall at the center of the building gave researchers ample space to stage prototypes and exhibitions, and wings of offices on either side of the hall were renovated to accommodate the Institute's vision of an "interdisciplinary research organism."

Successive drafts of the Institute's floorplan incrementally adapted the building to the structural clarity of the institutional diagram. Each space was developed in light of the essential activities of the Institute. For instance, the "laboratory" would be a machine shop for producing research prototypes, and the "information center" would provide a hard-wired connection to USC's mainframe computer and "include every possible medium of communication," according to its creator.

● Conference room of the Building Institute at the University of Southern California, outfitted with ashtrays, panoramic slide projection wall at rear, telephone and audio recording equipment at right; a microphone hangs at center, above the table.

74

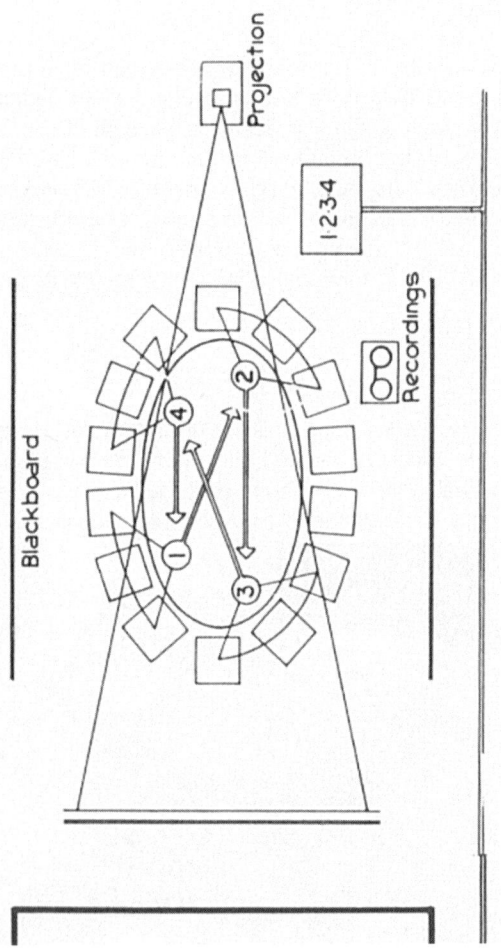

Projection

1 2 3 4

Recordings

Blackboard

But the conference room was the true heart of the Institute. Following the seminar protocols that Wachsmann had invented in the 1950s, structured discussions around the oblong table would be recorded and entered into the Institute's database for future reference. The ability to capture information as soon as it was broadcast allowed the Institute to close the feedback loop back upon itself, recapturing information as an asset to future research. The social functioning of the room was strictly planned in Wachsmann's curriculum charts, which include a seating plan for optimum discussion between teams. Like the Building Institute's other spaces, the conference room was designed to facilitate the production and transmission of information. Whether taking the form of models, drawings, lectures, photographs, films, or prototypes, the Institute's essential preoccupation was the circulation of information.

● Drawing of an ideal conference room set-up and seating arrangement for a "superteam" of four, three-person groups working collaboratively on a task. Each group would cycle through smaller tasks throughout the course of a larger project, thus ensuring that each problem is addressed by the complete range of expertise and creative viewpoints in any given team.

Maximizing the number of productive nodes enmeshed in the network was one strategy for raising the status of the research. Bauhaus founder Walter Gropius and design theorist Horst Rittel both made visits to the Institute, and Buckminster Fuller frequently stopped by on visits to Los Angeles during development of the "World Game" in the late 1960s. Ludwig Mies van der Rohe also visited once, and by one student's recollection, the ailing master had to be lifted upstairs to the Institute by means of a forklift in the armory hall. Fritz Haller, too, was a collaborator of the Institute from 1966–71, developing grid structures that anticipated his later commercial designs for building systems.

But the only project known to have been realized by the Institute was the Location Orientation Manipulator, "L.O.M.," a robotic arm designed by two doctoral students, John Bollinger and Xavier Mendoza. The purpose of the device was to study the "kinematics of prefabricated building," that is, the manipulation of objects in space. It was funded by a three-year grant from the Weyerhaeuser lumber corporation, and it marked the Institute's definitive move into "basic research." Defined by Vannevar Bush in 1945 as inquiry that "is performed without thought of practical ends," this type of work produced not solutions but "general knowledge and an understanding of nature and its laws."[2]

2   Vannevar Bush was director of the U.S. Office of Scientific Research and Development during Second World War. Vannevar Bush, "Science, the Endless Frontier," 1945.

Whereas the earlier study of structural systems for the California City City Hall was developed in the context an architectural project, the L.O.M. device had no such immediate applications. Rather, the creation of this instrument for studying the problems of building assembly was itself the research agenda.

● The L.O.M. project was completed in 1971, when doctoral students John Bollinger and Xavier Mendoza defended their joint dissertation.

Indeed, outside of the Institute, the L.O.M. had no useful purpose. The device was not sophisticated enough to be taken up by the building industry, and thus its sponsors could not exploit it for production. Eventually, the impressive device was disassembled, boxed up, and lost. But between 1967–71, the L.O.M. proved immeasurably useful to the Institute's protagonists. For Wachsmann, the device was the Institute's *raison d'etre,* a high-profile and big-budget project that justified his organization's continued existence. For the sponsors, it was an opportunity to ally their corporation with the cutting-edge of building science research at a prestigious university. For the graduate students Bollinger and Mendoza, the device was an expedient to their doctoral degrees. Common to all of these purposes, however, was the device's ability to yield alluring images.

Whether appearing in photographs in Weyerhaeuser's publicity materials, or in Bollinger and Mendoza's joint dissertation, or in Wachsmann's slide lectures, the L.O.M. was an object of distinguished aesthetic presence that rather resembled László Moholy-Nagy's "Light-Space Modulator" more than an experimental apparatus. As an object of considerable aesthetic quality but little value to either further research or applied use, the L.O.M. can be said to embody the Building Institute's central paradox: as Wachsmann's research agenda became more theoretically speculative, the value of his research to sponsors, whether government or corporate, diminished in kind.

● The Building Institute's first sponsored research funds were received August 21, 1967, in the form of a check for $40,000. The contribution represented the first of three years of support that the Institute would receive from Weyerhaeuser.

After completion of the L.O.M. project in 1971, the Institute would constantly struggle to justify its own existence as a venue for experimental work on building science and technology. The Institute had placed itself at odds with the prevailing dynamics of the Cold War research economy. First, by avoiding applied research, the Institute could not offer compelling arguments that would entice corporations to sponsor new projects. Second, Wachsmann's "hypothesis-free" ethos of experiment alienated him with respect to public sources of funding for scientific research. In response to questions about what could be gained by undertaking projects like the L.O.M., Wachsmann replied, "... my answer always was, that I did not know. But this was the same answer I would always give when I worked on any task. If I would know the solution or the purpose, I would not start at all."[3]

The Building Institute was shuttered for lack of funding in 1974, but not before Wachsmann had developed a teaching system that sought to standardize the production of knowledge and built a school to implement it. In the context of the architect's lifelong engagement with industrialization, the Institute represents the architect's most sophisticated proposal for architecture's alignment with science and industry.

3 Konrad Wachsmann, "The Future is Everything," in: unpublished autobiography manuscript, "1901 Timebridge 2001," consulted at the Akademie der Künste, Berlin, Konrad Wachsmann Archive, Wachsmann 2128.

That this confluence would take place on the grounds of a school resonated both with the program of the Bauhaus, as well as the emerging neoliberal transformation of the university, what President Eisenhower called in 1961 the "military-industrial-academic complex."

The case of the Building Institute is exceptional with respect to other organizations for building science in its time. It is unusual in that it was simultaneously unable to accede to the demands of the research economy, and yet it nevertheless fashioned itself after the model of scientific research laboratories in the university. Rather, the Institute sought to establish a pedagogical system whose parallel functions as didactic environment and as experimental laboratory would be coproductive. Whether in the Institute conference room or in the laboratory, new information would be produced, captured, and capitalized upon as the product of sponsored research. Students would train to become participants in this circular production of valuable knowledge, and in the process, their academic labor became the Institute's product.

● Drawings of L.O.M. components on a drawing board in the Building Institute workspace circa 1970. A partial prototype of the device can be seen near the corridor.

But Wachsmann's unerring faith in the value of design did not match the evaluative calculus of his would-be sponsors. Still, the architect's systematic transformation of pedagogical activity into an economically productive process pointed in the direction that building science laboratories, and academic science in general, would take after the 1970s. As was true in the case of the Building Institute and other university laboratories, physical space gathered the resources of the university—materiel and personnel —for the purpose of producing saleable research. In this respect, the Institute was established precisely on the historical fulcrum which saw a pivot from industrial forms of production to the post-industrial economy. Whereas Wachsmann's early-career efforts to develop prefabricated building systems sought to subsume architecture within industry, the Building Institute thus attempted to reconstitute *architecture itself* as a technological product produced by scientific labor.

Hangar / Atom

Konrad Wachsmann's "New Method of Construction" drawings of 1939 set the course for his future work on steel construction systems. Working with the structural engineer Paul
Weidlinger in 1944, Wachsmann began to develop the "Mobilar Structure" for the Atlas Aircraft Corporation. The system
was patented in 1945, retaining the key elements Wachsmann outlined several years earlier: a set of standard fully
reusable structural elements, and pin connections that could
be easily joined or released without destroying the parts.

Work on the structure continued at the Institute of Design in
Chicago, where it caught the attention of the U.S. Air Force.
The subsequent project was a commission particular to the
Cold War era: a demountable system for aircraft hangars.
It took shape in a series of impressive models produced by
graduate students at the school. Based on the space frame
technique, the structure used triangular trusses to cantilever
over vast expanses of space used to maintain the largest
airplanes in the Air Force fleet.

The project was never realized, but the uninterrupted "universal
space" of the hangar set a spatial ideal for the whole generation
of architects. From Buckminster Fuller's geodesic domes to visionary works after 1960 by the likes of Constant Nieuwenhuys,
Yona Friedman, Cedric Price and others. Tubular structures
opened the possibility of reimagined lifestyles of continuous
mobility and free association within a fluid social community.
This vision offered a radical move beyond the separations of
traditional buildings or the version offered by General Panel.

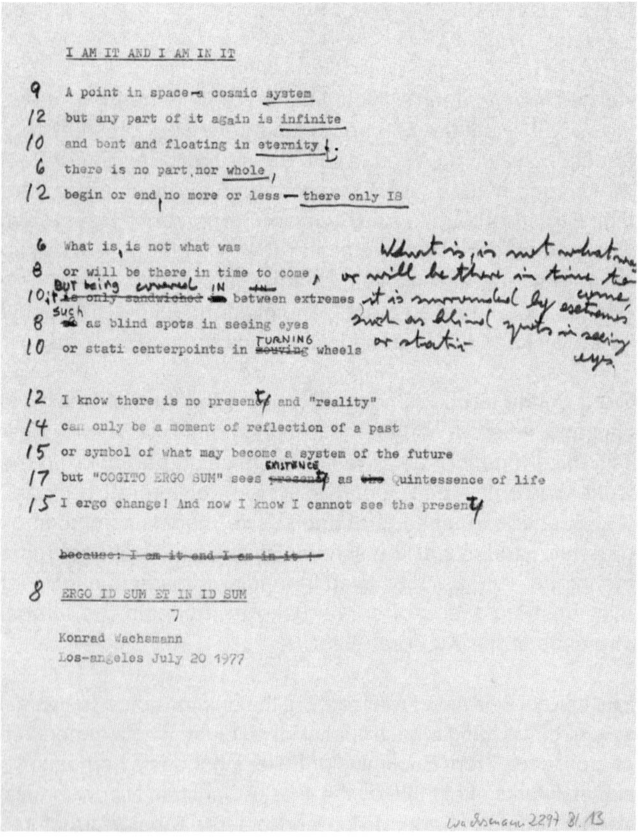

I AM IT AND I AM IN IT

9   A point in space—a cosmic system

12   but any part of it again is infinite

10   and bent and floating in eternity.

6   there is no part nor whole,

12   begin or end no more or less — there only IS

6   What is is not what was

8   or will be there in time to come,

10   BUT being ~~it is only sandwiched~~ cramped in between extremes

8   such ~~as~~ as blind spots in seeing eyes

10   or stati centerpoints in ~~moving~~ TURNING wheels

(handwritten revision in right margin):
What is is not what was
or will be there in time to come,
it is surrounded by extremes
such as blind spots in seeing
eyes
or static

12   I know there is no present and "reality"

14   can only be a moment of reflection of a past

15   or symbol of what may become a system of the future

17   but "COGITO ERGO SUM" sees ~~present~~ as ~~the~~ quintessence of life

15   I ergo change! And now I know I cannot see the present

~~because: I am it and I am in it !~~

8   ERGO ID SUM ET IN ID SUM

        7

Konrad Wachsmann
Los-angeles July 20 1977

Wachsmann 2297 81/13

● July 20, 1977 draft of "I am it and I am in it," a poem by
Konrad Wachsmann.

In Los Angeles 1977, the late Konrad Wachsmann sketched multiple versions of a poem which he headlined "I am it and I am in it" or just simply with "I am." In total, there is an archived stack of roughly 32 sketches with variations and iterations of the very same poem—mostly handwritten or typewritten, with the latter ones frequently annotated and reworked by hand.

It is unclear why Wachsmann was drawn to occupy himself with a poem over the course of a couple of months (according various date specifications). Only a fraction of the stack reveals an additional note, namely an homage dedicated to a certain "Master Charles" for his 70th Birthday, which referred to his contemporary, Charles Eames, who turned 70 in June the very same year. And besides, only the first paragraph of the three-part poem is indicated as an homage to Eames on the already very few sketches where he is even mentioned. This means that for the following two paragraphs Wachsmann didn't have a specific person in mind to whom he was devoting his lyrical efforts. Therefore, it seems almost as if he tried obsessively to frame a certain self-explanation or even self-justification through the means of a free and associative lyrical expression like poetry.

As pathetic or vulnerable as his attempt might appear today, it nevertheless reveals a diverse and multifaceted reading of his architectural "back catalog," especially in regard to his notorious experiments with tubular steel structure systems. Amongst them, one of Wachsmann's most celebrated and influential works is the project of an aircraft hangar commissioned by the U.S Air Force in the early 1950s. Here, the architect developed a massive network of interconnected, tubular steel structure systems that could create vast spaces for the housing of large aircraft. Due to its fundamental functional necessity, it is first and foremost an almost floating spatial structure, and second a detailed study of a part-to-whole organization, where multiple steel rods are connected in order to create strong nodal points for supporting again vast spatial arrangements. The result is a systematic approach from the concentration on specific detail solutions to fully organized and almost endless interconnected structures. Hence the project celebrated Wachsmann internationally in the late 1950s as a specialist of so called "space-frame" structures. In 1964 he founded the Building Research Division at the University of Southern California in Los Angeles, where he further expanded the idea of wide-spanned roof structures, which in turn led to projects like the California Civic City Center.

Even though Wachsmann's modular "space-frame" experiments are highly technological in spirit, there is plenty of room for interpretation, notably from the soon-to-arrive avant–gardists of visionary architecture. As Mark Wigley pointed out, "Fuller's demonstration of an Octet-truss at MoMA; Constant Nieuwenhuys's 'wide world web' New Babylon; and Eckhard Schultze-Fielitz's Space City each … was influenced by Konrad Wachsmann's enormous Airline Hangar for the U.S. Air Force that was first published in 1954." In this regard, Wachsmann and his search for structural universality influenced a group of architects, artists and designers in order to conceptually expand on the social possibilities inherent in the space frame systems – especially in order to project new societal forms of sharing space.

One significant quality, often overlooked in this discourse, is the role of ambiguity. On the one hand, the representation of endless open structures generated not only a claim for universality from the single part to the whole organization, but also became food for thought and freedom of experimentation for others. And this can be traced back to Wachsmann and his attempt to express a certain view through poetry. Because to choose poetry as a form of expression means to allow ambiguity and consequently to allow a certain degree of open interpretation of the written subject. While the hangar proposed a paradigmatic interpretation of freespace, the poem proposed the interpretation of free thought. In the end his hangar project wasn't realized, and maybe neither was the poem, according to the dozens of sketches left behind. What remains are just structures, probably somewhere in space.

On the following pages, a draft of "I'm it and I'm in it," is juxtaposed with archival images of his experiments in tubular steel construction systems, such as the "Mobilar Structure" for the Atlas Aircraft Corporation and the hangar for the U.S. Air Force, as well as the California City Civic Center.

A point in space is a cosmic <u>system</u>

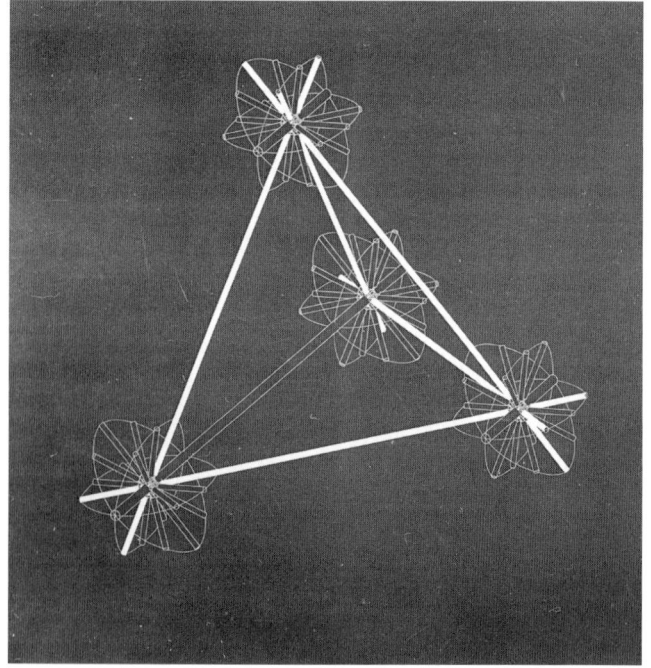

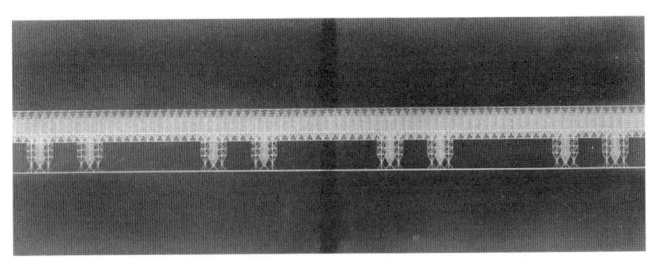

but any part of it again is <u>infinite</u>

and bent and floating in <u>eternity;</u>

there is no part nor <u>whole,</u>
begin or end, no more or less –
<u>*there only IS*</u>

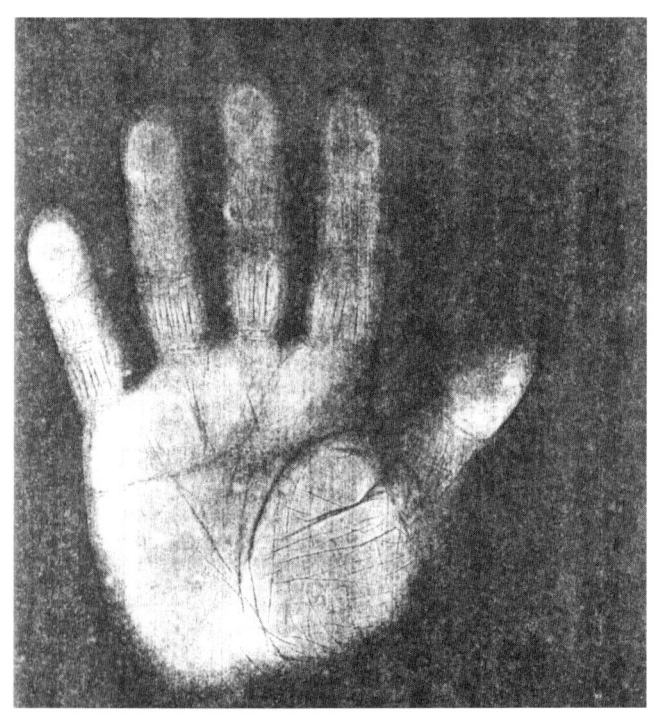

What is, is not what was
or will be there in time to come,

it is surrounded by extremes

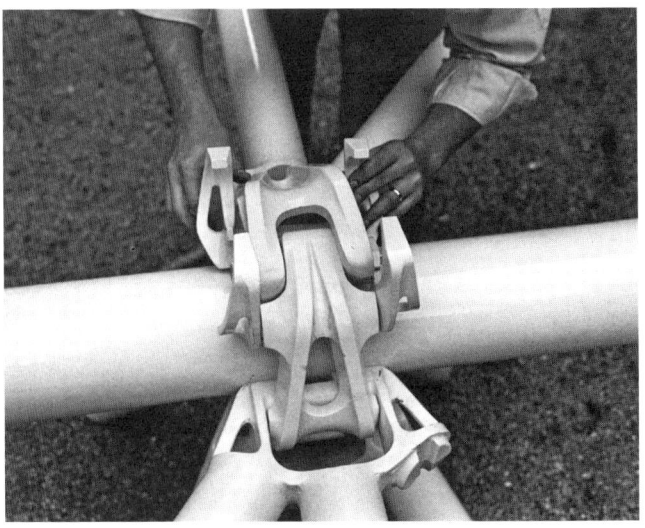

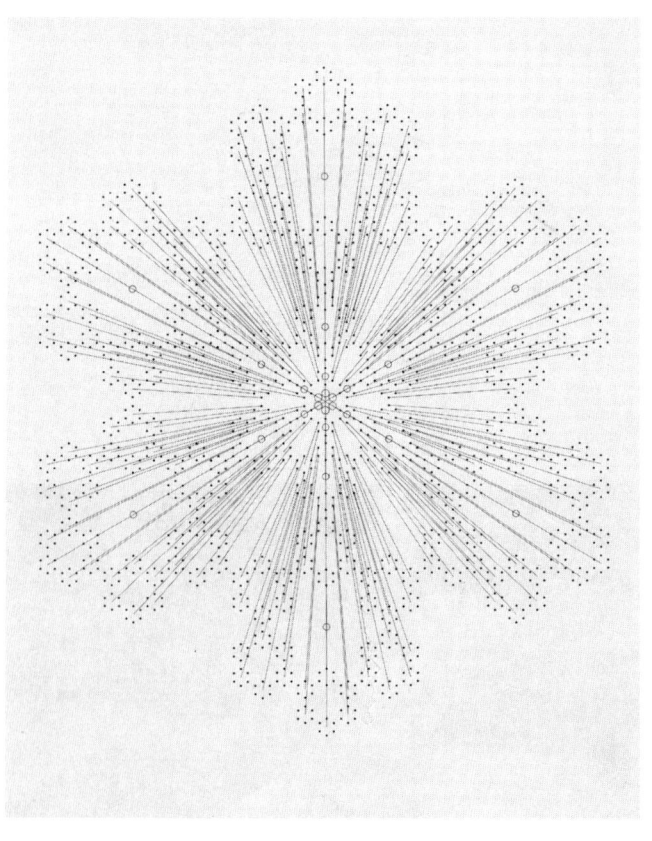

such as blind spots in seeing eyes

or static centerpoints in turning wheels

*I know there is no present, and "reality"
can be a moment in reflection of a past*

or symbolic for what may become a system of the <u>future</u>

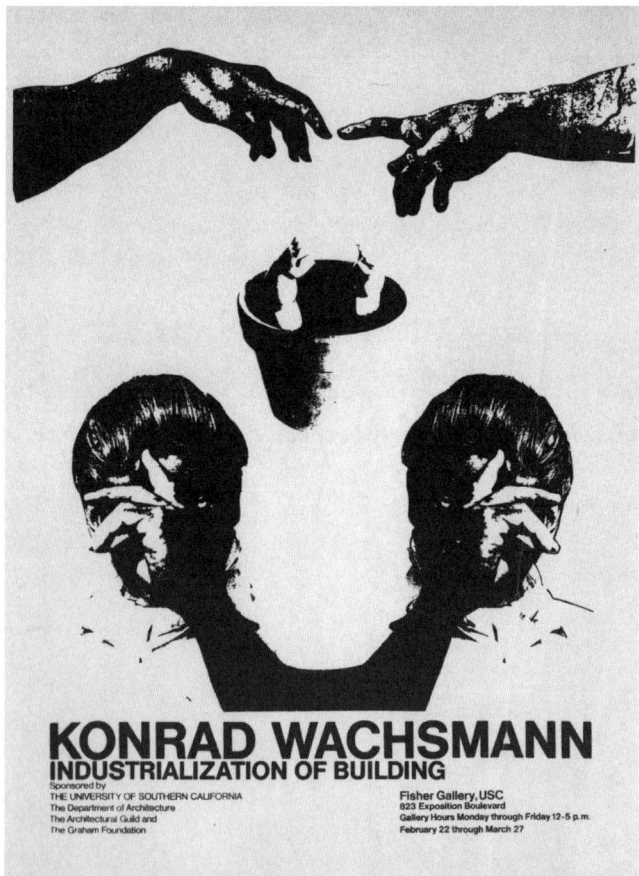

KONRAD WACHSMANN
INDUSTRIALIZATION OF BUILDING

Sponsored by
THE UNIVERSITY OF SOUTHERN CALIFORNIA
The Department of Architecture
The Architectural Guild and
The Graham Foundation

Fisher Gallery, USC
823 Exposition Boulevard
Gallery Hours Monday through Friday 12-5 p.m.
February 22 through March 27

but "COGITO ERGO SUM" sees existence as the Quintessence of <u>life</u> I ergo change! And now I know that I cannot see the <u>present,</u>

ERGO ID SUM ET IN ID SUM
[I'm it and I'm in it]

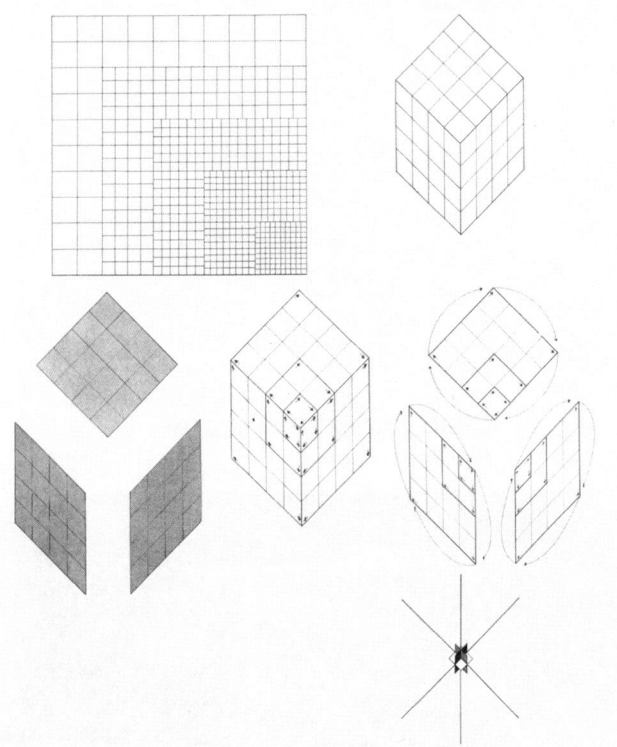

● Wachsmann drew 13 diagrams (1–6 above) that illustrated his approach to building, published later in his book *The
Turning Point of Building, Structure and Design,* 1959.

Signs and their visualizations have always played an important role in the negotiation of social norms surrounding groups of individuals. Adrian Frutiger chose to start his book, *Man and His Signs* (1978) with Albert Einstein's words: "The word or the language, written or spoken, does not seem to matter at all in the mechanism of my thought process. The basic psychic elements of thinking are certain signs and more or less clear images that can be reproduced and combined *as desired*." On this basis, I would like to speculate on the work of Konrad Wachsmann, analyzing two particular objects in his work: a series of system diagrams and the final version of the wedge connector, both originating in 1947.

The objects: Parallel to the construction of the General Panel factory, which was expected to produce the Packaged House in a fully automated environment, Wachsmann created thirteen system diagrams. The series begins with a single flat square. The square is subsequently multiplied to form a three-dimensional cube. In the next steps, the cube's surfaces shift and pierce into each other. What we observe here is a creation of three-dimensional from the two-dimensional. This transition forms the basis for a Packaged House. In it, all the structural differences within the building—such as those between wall, floor and ceiling—disappear. Instead, a modular structure becomes a key element of this systematic construction. As Wachsmann writes of the system in 1942, "All panels, whether for floor, walls, partitions, ceilings, or roofs, are structurally identical, and all connections, whether one-, two-, three- or four-ways, whether horizontal or vertical, are in all respects identical. This allows for interchangeability of all parts and, consequently, for a thorough application of mass production techniques."

Wachsmann completed the concept for Packaged House with the graphical reflections and, over time, he implemented a similar-looking "sculpture"—an object highlighting its symbolic terms—as an integral part of the houses: the universal connector. The first version of the connector from 1939 was angular. But in the same year of the American nuclear attack on Hiroshima and Nagasaki, 1945, he rounded off the edges.

● Building components are understood in their dynamic relations. With the ninth diagram, the series evolves in a symbol for Wachsmann's general theory of construction.

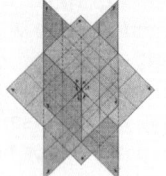 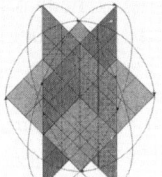 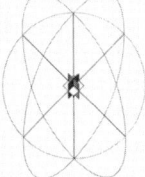

● The axial grid allows for the design of infinite variations.

● The reason the wedge connector was rounded off in 1945 remains unclear.

The change in shape and size to a more "atomic" design was confirmed in his design decision of 1947, when he stretched the proportions of the connector towards a round sphere. A sphere which strongly reminds us of a the archaic idea of the atom which goes back to Giordano Bruno's drawings of 1591.

Scientific representations: The turn of the 20th century marked the beginning of the "atomic age." With newly developed instruments and calculations, new atomic models appeared and the power contained in the tiniest elements of matter became visible. The world's first nuclear reactor was put into operation in a laboratory at the University of Chicago in 1942. The production of the atomic bomb and later the hydrogen bomb, as well as the production of radioisotopes and of atomic electricity, began with the help of nuclear fission. The atomic model became a crucial symbol for a whole generation, from science to pop culture. It promised scientific breakthroughs, resolution of energy scarcity while providing for the supposed final understanding of the universe. At the same time, it hid the risks of total annihilation that its power meant for human culture.

The first scientist to acquire knowledge about of the "precise form" of the atoms might be Ernest Rutherford in 1908. In exchange with Niels Bohr, they developed in the following years a picture of the atom which looked like a miniature solar system. The negative electrons revolve around the nucleus like planets around the sun, occasionally jumping from one orbit to the other. The infinitely great and the infinitely small, the electron and the planet, went reeling round.

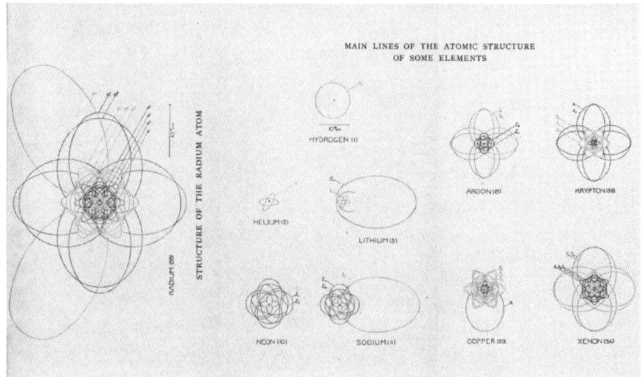

● Niels Bohr's theory of the atom as a miniature solar system saw principles of the biggest in the smallest.

In 1922 Bohr received the Nobel prize, the year before he had drawings made which represented the orbits for selected atoms and were published widely in Europe. In the U.S., the older imaginary types of cubic configuration of the outer electrons by Lewis-Langmuir were widely presented in parallel to the newer theory of the orbits by Bohr.

Subsequently, the legendary debate between Einstein and Bohr took place facilitating negotiations on the model of the atom within the world of science. While Einstein believed in a unified theory elegantly explaining the universe, Bohr said there is no access to ultimate reality and was satisfied or tempted by an enormity of unseen possibilities.

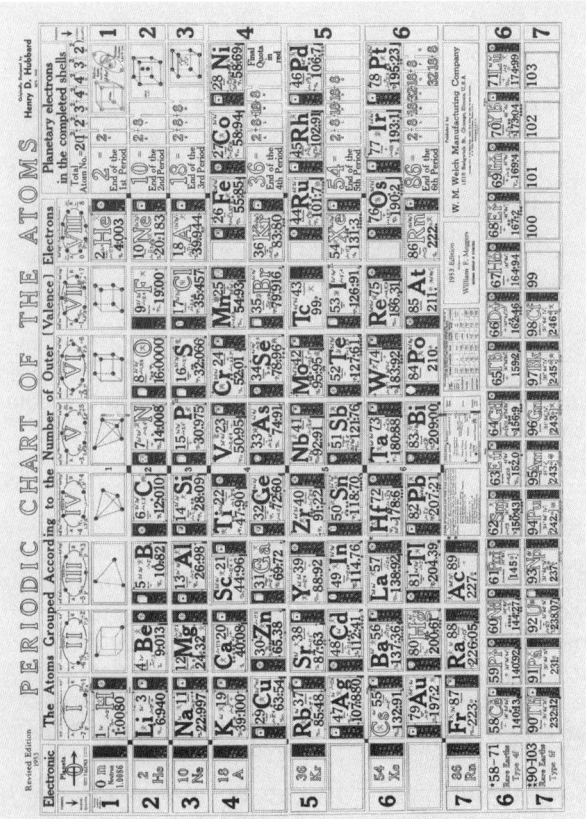

● Wachsmann collected scientific representations that informed his designs.

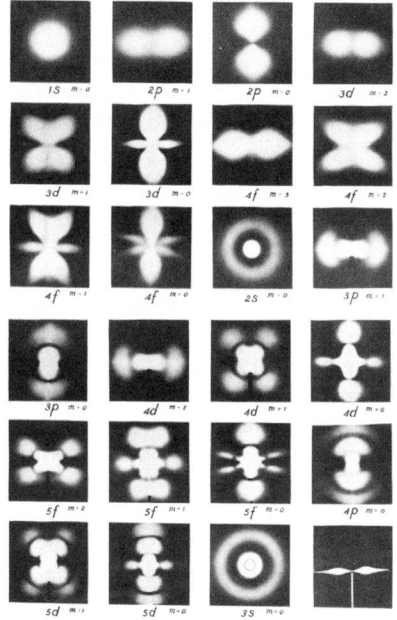

● Representations of electron clouds contributed to understanding of the unpredictability of nature.

From 1925 onwards, the Rutherford-Bohr model was super-seded by more accurate physical theories. Precisely defined circular paths were replaced by diffuse clouds, visualized in 1931: Quantum mechanics implied that microscopic particles such as electrons move discontinuously and seemingly ran-domly.

Over the last 100 years, the model of the building blocks of reality has changed and evolved continuously: atoms, elementary particles, quarks, strings, loops. Every form became documented, discussed and gradually influence not only scientific worldview but also culture in its broader scope. Those models and notions coexist and are thought and taught side by side to better understand new things.

Shifting to popularity: The Bohr-Rutherford atom model be-came popular and widely recognizable in the following de-cades. With the symbol so ubiquitous, key questions arise: Which stories in the sign are hidden and which of its aspects are exposed? Who feels connected with such symbol?

The Packaged House system was mainly funded by the U.S. government, in order to provide demountable housing, barracks, which could be used to house the army—an army of workers. Wachsmann was designing for a very specifi-cally understood U.S. citizen in reply to the commission from the State and the Army. As mentioned, Wachsmann started reshaping the wedge connector in 1945. Whereas in Japan the atomic explosion became a horrific reality of mass murder, in the U.S. the distanced victorious and heroic perspective took over. Wachsmann's introduction of the symbolic shape of an atom might be read in the U.S. as an early sign of victory — and overall as a symbol for the successful combination of military and science.

Wachsmann clearly understood the dependence of industrial society on energy and access to energy as a precondition for industrialized building. This subject was issued throughout the country, as well as the solution was advertised. Belief in unlimited access to energy through breakthroughs in atomic science was helplessly euphoric, as when German officials declared in 1956: "It means that we will soon be able to put a teaspoon of nuclear energy into our car and drive years without refilling."[1] The government's decision to use nuclear energy was a logical consequence of "technology policy," which ruthlessly put economic and military growth above all other human interests. Machines have to be fed with energy; in the second of his seven theses, Wachsmann claims: "THE MACHINE IS THE TOOL OF OUR TIME, and cause of those effects which characterize the accepted order of our society."[2]

1 Gerhard Löwenthal and Josef Hausen: *Wir werden durch Atome leben,* Introduction by Dr. Otto Hahn and Franz-Josef Strauß (by that time German Federal Minister of Nuclear Affairs, 1956, 17.
2 Konrad Wachsmann, "Seven Theses," Konrad Wachsmann Archive, Akademie der Künste, Berlin, Wachsmann, 466.

Shifting to design: At this point I would propose a close look at Wachsmann's diagram No. 75. Previously in the book, he presents historical diagrams illustrating proportion: The Vitruvian Man, where the male human is used as a reference for scale; the "golden ratio," the measure for the antiquity; finally the Gothic master diagram as the mystical standard of the late Medieval era. After all those diagrams No. 75 appear as a representation for industrialized building. Its caption says: "Symbol of measure, movement and time, into which every imaginary form can be inserted in the system of an assumed relationship." Therefore, what Wachsmann created here is an ideogram that abstracts the idea of how to build in the world of mass production.

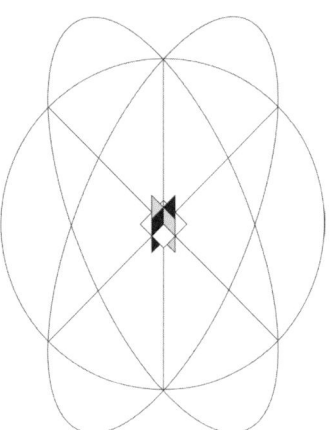

● Diagram No. 75.

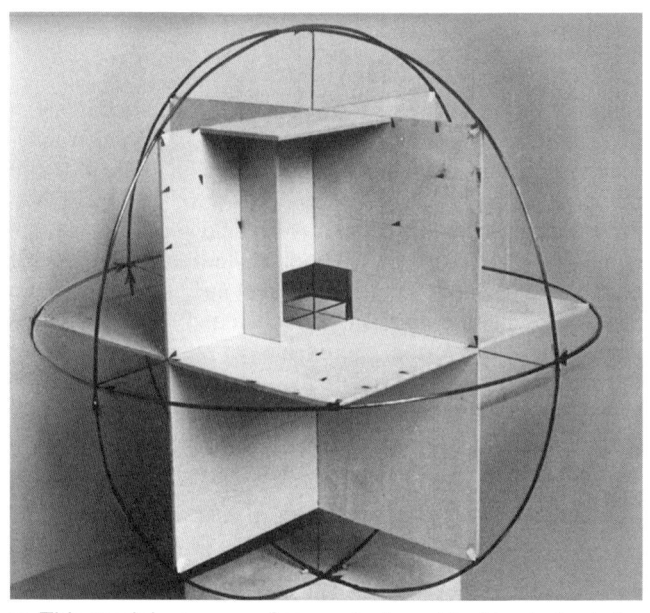

● This model was one of many designed by his students for the Lausanne workshop, 1959.

Diagram No. 75 suggests the cube as elementary particle of this methodical design process. Consequently, from Wachsmann's book layouts to his architectural structures, they can be observed as the basic unit of his design. He said: "Here, for instance, we have a cube. … With an object like this there is repetition all the time …,"[3] and: "Following the conditions of industrialization, by multiplication of cell and element, the structure shall find its form,"[4] Wachsmann introduces here not merely a new formal expression but rather he translated the scientific discoveries of the modern age into architecture. While introducing this new thinking, he maintains the belief that the future can only be achieved if the whole society will be educated on the new developments—starting with his university students.

Wachsmann held the architectural class in the Academy of Fine Arts Salzburg, from 1956 to 1960. His teachings made an important impact on Vienna's design scene. One of his students remembered: "… planning decisions could not be based on 'ideas' but would have to be worked out in a strict methodological way," because they "multiply indefinitely on the scale of industrial production … Fundamentals and assumptions were defined that, each analyzed individually, made the design process a sequence of logical decisions."[5]

3   Konrad Wachsmann, "Building In Our Time," 1957, 17.
4   Konrad Wachsmann, "Seven Theses."
5   Eva Kuß: *Hermann Czech. Architekt in Wien,* Park Books, Zurich, 2018, 70-74.

● Students built this structure during the Lausanne workshop, 1959.

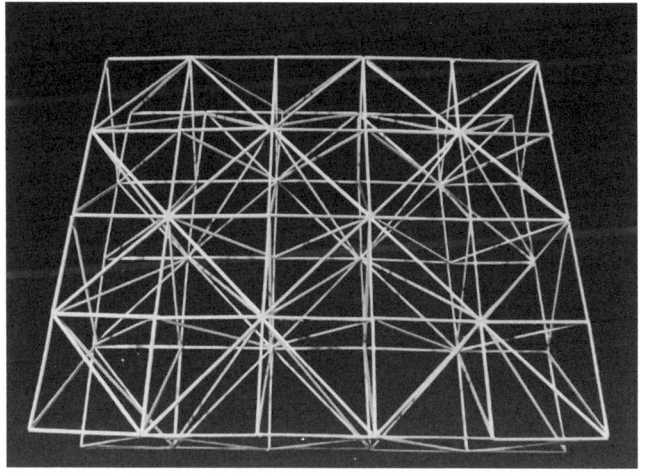

● New and old architectural concepts seen side by side.

In the seminars, the students explored the building of different structures that clearly refer to the chemical table of Hubbard. In 1958, they developed a flexible building for an art, science and technology center. The design idea, already present in the Packaged House, is underlined by the fact that the model of the cultural center can be packed in a box, revealing a grid and sets of standardized rectangular objects, that, as atoms, together give shape to the building. For his approach to architecture, in 1974 Wachsmann received a nomination for the National American Institute of Architects Medal for Research.

● Reflecting the periodic chart of atoms, this box allowed people to build different architectural structures from elements.

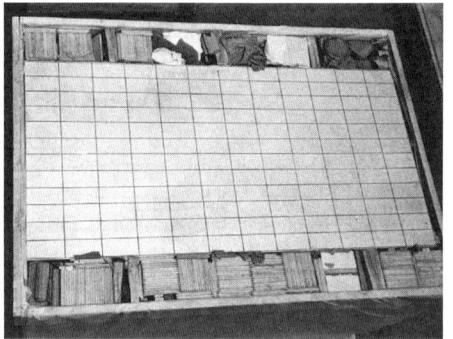

● Model photographed by a student in the Salzburg Summer Academy in 1960.

Wachsmann stayed close to the development of physics through his longtime friendship with Albert Einstein and other scientists met during his extensive travels in the following decades. He built a collection of scientific instruments and teaching materials. His lifelong connection to institutions of the U.S. government attracts special attention. In those years, the U.S. military—Wachsmann's major client—keeps up and supports groundbreaking science, often regardless of costs and morality, to develop new technologies. Derived from wartime experience, the use of computational information technologies and the "mixed-team approach" of research and development can be easily recognized in Wachmann's own practice.

"Scientific communication" begins in the service of science in order to liberate the world from myths, now "scientific communication" itself works to disseminate modern myths. As a "science communicator," Wachsmann's work methods and his architectural concepts align with the myth of the orderly world: the big and the small work identically, just like in the atomic model of the mini-solar system that he quoted. He was one of the first to create a symbol from the Bohr-Rutherford atom model by shifting it into his own context. In this geometric vision, nature appears as a calculable thing, with the idea of linear planning of probabilities.

Vice versa: Wachsmann models and drawings have endured as material evidence for his thinking and projects, enabling us to discuss those ideas today. The visual language that he mobilized and promoted was based on his fascination with science—and in consequence a physical perspective on the world that implies: everything and everybody is build by the same particles. As complex forms of knowledge and communication, visualizations are accessible to many and enable a broad audience to debate on them. Wachsmann offered a re-integration of science and society. And, vice versa, by doing so he was able to claim a scientific status for his design practice. His visualizations can provoke emotional feedback, as only embodied knowledge can lead to shaping the future.

Slowly, the ideas of his time are passing. Contemporary discussions on liquidity, rhizomes and fluid forms accompany negotiations of other forms of living and designing. Design research as a methodology takes a leading role in this process. There is a need in society to ask designers to search for knowledge and results accommodating a wide spectrum of discussions. Yet, design should not absorb social insecurities, as technology did in the past decades. Sharing knowledge openly, across fields and borders, could act against such processes as a counterbalance. As design theorists Anthony Dunne and Fiona Raby affirmed already in 2007, design can place new scientific and technological developments within imaginary but believable everyday situations, allowing us to debate the implications of different futures. This shift from thinking about applications to implications creates a need for new design roles, contexts and methods. From this perspective, the most beautiful thing is the fact that Wachsmann's models were never built. We can therefore see how design, as words, as a note on a piece of paper, as a mere prototype, can influence the world we live in.

Table / Education

In 1949, Wachsmann left General Panel Corporation, which was by then well on its way to bankruptcy. That same year, Serge Chermayeff invited Wachsmann to join the faculty of the Institute of Design in Chicago. He was appointed to teach in the newly-formed Advanced Building Research Division.

Wachsmann developed an experimental pedagogy that diverged from both the Bauhaus-inspired curriculum of the Institute and the professional training program of the architecture department, devised by Ludwig Mies van der Rohe. The Research Division also deviated in its curriculum structure. Instead of academic semesters or project-oriented design studios, students and specialists would come together in the context of a single goal and for as long as funding allowed.

Wachsmann characterized his work as "basic research" on general themes rather than "applied research" on narrowly-defined problems. His transdisciplinary perspective was influenced by the emerging field of cybernetics, a subject established by mathematician Norbert Wiener only a year before Wachsmann started teaching in Chicago. Cybernetics attracted mathematicians, philosophers, social scientists, neuro-scientists, and some artists and designers with the promise of transforming scientific understandings of consciousness and communication. Government research funding fueled a Cold War-era technology race and nurtured the field. Cybernetics revolutionized the development of midcentury technologies of production and destruction, and although the Building Research Division never fully applied cybernetic methods, it did internalize the logic of cybernetics in its systematic approaches to teaching and collaborative research.

TABULA RASA: KONRAD WACHSMANN'S UNIVERSALISM AFTER THE UNIVERSAL CONNECTOR
EZGI ISBILEN

The demise of the Packaged House enterprise that was founded on the universal connector marks a turning point in its architect's career. While the Packaged House captured the architectural imagination of its time, and its promise of delivering affordable mass-produced housing by intelligent design that eliminates all potential problems at the drawing table still inspires many, Wachsmann's career after his quest for the holy grail of a universal connector escapes most accounts of post-war architectural discourse except appearances of spectacular images of notable projects like the United States Air Force Hangar (1951). The scope of his teaching lacks cultural presence. Wachsmann's own book *Turning Point of Building* includes a preview, but only covers its first decade, until the book's publication in 1959. The three decades of Wachsmann's teaching career, the networks of ideas it engaged and produced remain uncharted. The table section of our exhibit offered a preview that I further extend here.

Wachsmann's departure from General Panel Corporation and his transition to teaching may resemble a withdrawal, however his teaching career lacked neither in aspiration, nor in its commitment to standardization and the idea of universality. On the contrary, his new route was driven by the epiphany he had through his previous work in practice, which Wachsmann describes in his unpublished autobiography "Timebridge" (1981):

"I started the basic design for this housing system under obscure conditions in Europe […] convinced that this approach represented the only possible way to deal with modern housing. I came to the United States and re-designed the whole system in Lincoln with Walter Gropius. We built several test houses and finally a gigantic factory. I learned enough to understand that the principle in itself was wrong. And when I wanted to create the real product, it was too late."

Motivated by such a revelation, Wachsmann started his teaching career with a *tabula rasa*. While he used his connections and reputation as the architect of industrialization to secure commissions to sustain his research and teaching activities, his oeuvre shows an evident shift of emphasis from "construction" to "computation." One of the earliest projects taken up by the Advanced Building Division, which Wachsmann founded in Chicago as a joint department between the Illinois Institute of Technology and the Institute of Design, was the "Modular Coordination Classification System" (1951-52) commissioned by the Federal Housing Agency for advanced research in construction of mass-housing projects. Wachsmann and his students developed an apparatus built on the principles of Herman Hollerith's "tabulating machine;" using its method of information processing with punch cards, but adapting the categories to building systems, materials and components to capture all relevant information in one reference system, and to make it instantly accessible.

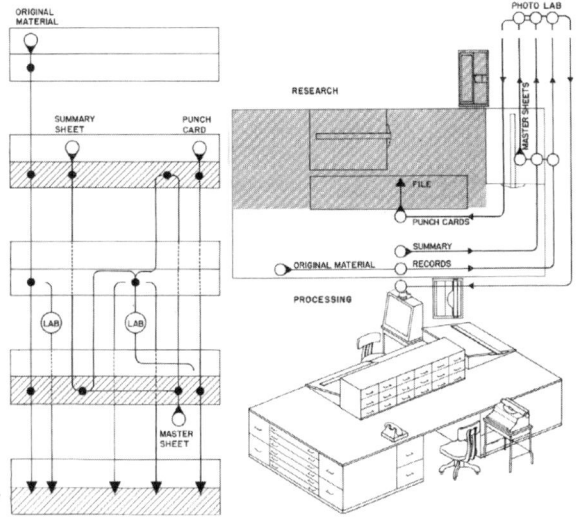

● "Modular Coordination Classification System".

● Punch card used in Herman Hollerith's tabulating
machine, circa 1895.

● Herman Hollerith's Tabulating Machine (center) with the punch for entering data (left), and the sorting box for sorting the cards for further analysis (right), circa 1890.

Before they became a medium to store information, punch cards were used to code instructions for machinery. They were either discarded at the end of the operation or reused for an identical operation. Wachsmann may have encountered this technology in its earlier form through his experience with prefabrication in Germany and in the U.S. However, the apparatus they developed had a greater scope than any linear operation. It was "an information machine" to assist designers in managing "the complexity of environmental and structural constraints" by providing "ready-made rational decisions."[13]

13 John Harwood, "The Rational, International Occult: Konrad Wachsmann and the Experimental Digitization of Architecture" in *Chicagoisms: The City as Catalyst for Architectural Speculation,* Park Books, Zurich, 2013, 62–75.

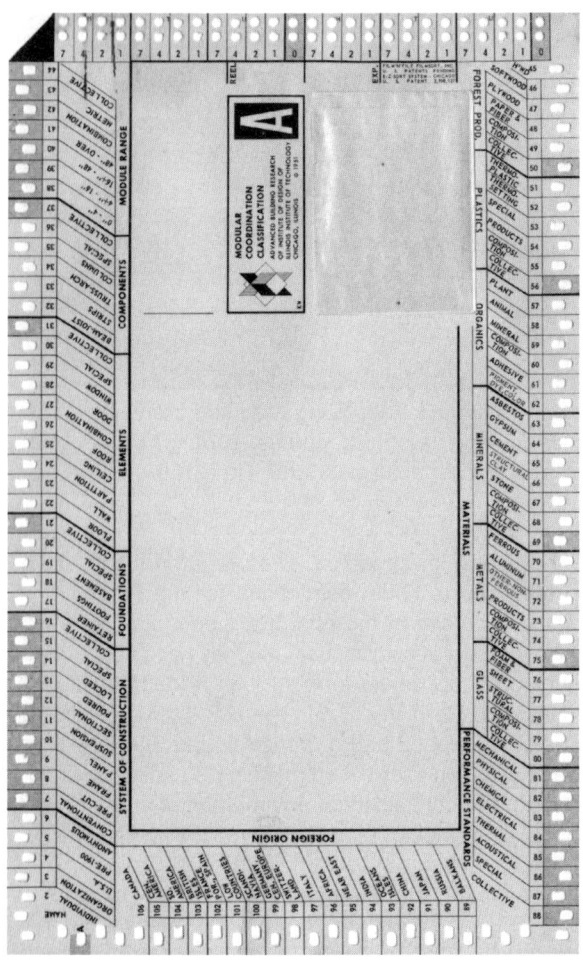

● Modular Coordination Classification Punchcard, 1951.

There are various historical precedents of such an undertaking such as Giulio Camillo's "Memory Theater" in the 16th century, and the *Encyclopédie* in the 18th century. Otto Neurath's *International Encyclopedia of Unified Science* (1938-69) from Wachsmann's own time was created with similar ideas of incorporating secularized, scientific, value-free facts in an accessible format. In retrospect we see that this was a spectacular dead end. But as historian David Hollinger states "the path to this dead end tells us much about the intellectual life of the most science-inspired intellectuals in the United States during the middle decades of the twentieth century."[14] It also gives us insight about our time. The dream of integrating all relevant information about a building project in a singular accessible format lingers in the field of architecture, most prominently in Building Information Modeling (BIM).

The apparatus Wachsmann and his students designed shows Wachsmann's skills as an architect and earlier as a cabinetmaker. Unlike Hollerith's machine, whose components were individual pieces of various sizes, connected by cables like a group of organs without a body, Wachsmann's apparatus integrates drawing equipment, filing cabinets, a punch card sorter, and a projector in the form of a composite table. The shape of the table attests to the cyclical nature of the process of continuous cataloging of an ever-growing database.

14 David A. Hollinger, "The Unity of Knowledge and the Diversity of Knowers: Science as an Agent of Cultural Integration in the United States Between the Two World Wars," *Pacific Historical Re*view, vol. 80, No. 2, May 2011, 211-230.

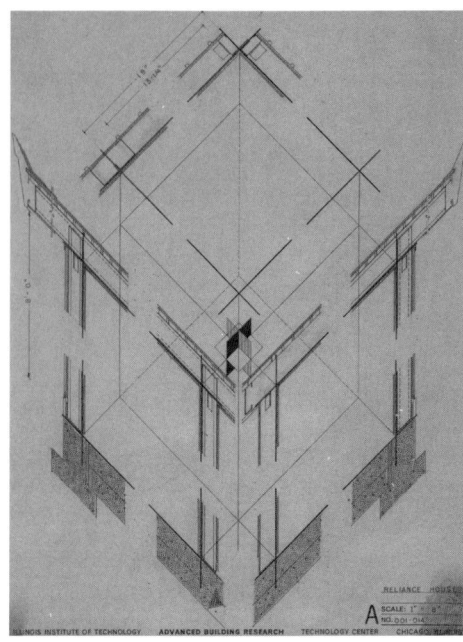

● Drawing of the Reliance House coded in the graphic representational system of the Modular Coordination Classification System.

In their attempt to record the data in various forms Wachsmann and his students added a window to the punch card to include microfilm. This allowed including data in the form of texts or drawings, which did not easily lend themselves in the categories that lined the punch card. While the addition of microfilm expanded the capacity of punch cards in registering data, it still fell short of its scope. Any building project requires various kinds of drawings conveying different kinds of information. Plans and sections show the spatial organization, size and relationship of various components of buildings in relations to each other. Detail drawings reveal tectonic and material character of buildings. Yet another set of drawings show the infrastructure of pipes, cords, ducts, locations of lighting fixtures and plugs. The detached logic of categorization did not suit the complexity of architectural production. At this point, Wachsmann invented a technique of representation embedded in the punch card but followed a slightly different mode of operation.

The method was based on an axonometric drawing showing an abstracted building cross-section with walls, floors and ceilings, the layer of materials they are composed of, how they are connected to each other at the corners, and how the whole arrangement connects to the ground. Following the pre-configured categories of the punch card, the relevant information was refined into a singular image. While some scholars question Wachsmann's technical comprehension of the logic of data processing using punch cards and its efficiency, what makes this early experiment of applying cybernetics in architecture interesting is its acuteness in interpreting it in architectural terms by spatializing what is essentially a process, and by translating the process into a graphic representational system.

Rational decision-making, which assumes the existence of an optimal design, is at the heart of Wachsmann's teaching. In addition to his work at the Advanced Building Division, Wachsmann also taught intermittently at HfG Ulm and Salzburg International Summer Academy. He organized a number of workshops around the world that accompanied his lectures and/or traveling exhibitions. To accommodate his mobility, he developed an algorithmic teaching model that can be implemented in different settings with varying number of students in multiples of three, ideally twenty-one.

He divided the participants in groups of three, and sub-divided the design problem into as many tasks as the number of student groups. Wachsmann met with the students regularly. Groups presented their work on the task before passing it on to the next group in order and taking up the one before them. The system facilitated iterative substitution until each group practiced every task and each task was designed with the contribution of each participant. While this distributed, iterative process did not always produce the result in the proposed time frame, and at times lasted three times longer, its results still inspired students. Hermann Czech, who attended Wachsmann's class in Salzburg International Summer Academy in 1958, recalls that "[i]n the end, as if miraculously, an object was generated."[15] While Czech confesses that eventually it was Wachsmann who made the decisions, as he gave logical reasons no one could doubt, this was imperceptible to the students. Wachsmann diagrammed his algorithm a number of times, marking the order of operations on the plan view of a table, around which the operation takes place, correlated with a timetable.

15 Marco Pogacnik, "Konrad Wachsmann and the teamwork concept in Salzburg: A Conversation with Fredrich Kurrent and Herman Czech," in: *Konrad Wachsmann and the* Grapewine Structure, eds. Marianne Burckhalter and Christian Sumi, Park Books, Zurich, 2018, 136.

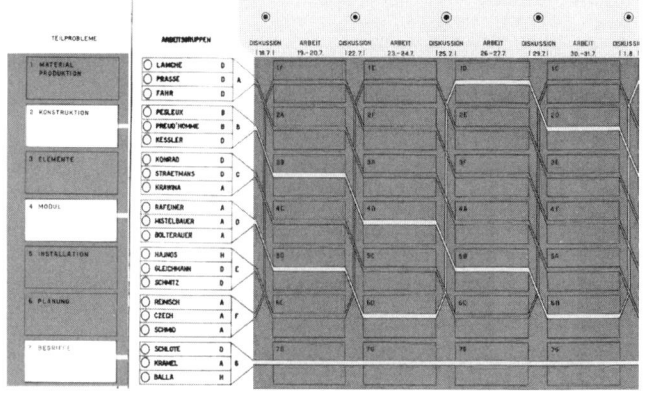

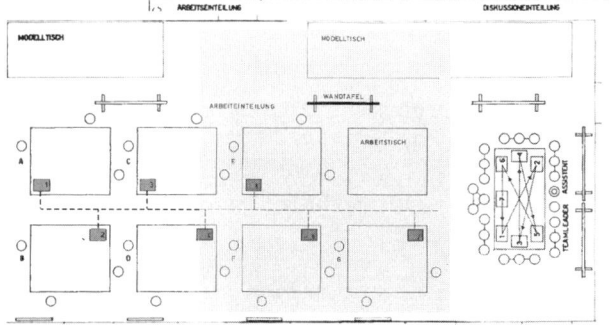

● Process diagram of the Salzburg International Summer School. Room plan correlated with timetable.

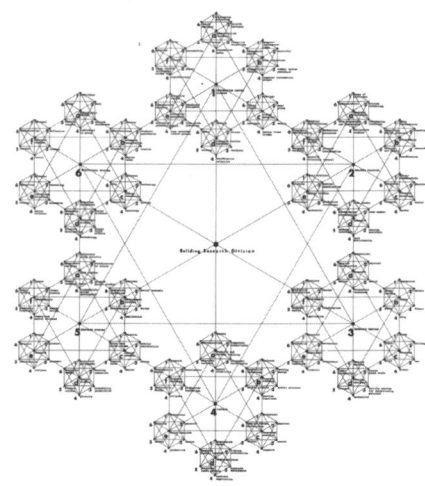

● Diagram of the distribution of activities of Building Research Institute, Arts & Architecture, May 1967.

● Expansion diagram of the Interdisciplinary Center, Arts & Architecture, May 1967.

Wachsmann used the algorithmic model throughout his teaching career. In the 1960s, at the University of Southern California, he radically scaled it up. Similar to the ever-changing students in his algorithmic process, he designated cellular units of "a constantly expanding interdisciplinary center." Wachsmann's "Predictions" published in *AIA Journal* (March 1972) included the absorption of existing departmental structures by the new interdisciplinary center, which will compose "an entirely new system of higher learning" and "will merge in a universal interdisciplinary forum of a *universitas*." The organization is clearest in his proposal for the Building Division, which is a hexagon composed of six sub-divisions of (1) information center and library, (2) teacher training, (3) research and testing, (4) faculty, (5) educational studies and (6) graduate studies. The subdivisions are designed to resonate. For instance, the educational studies would review the graduate studies, and their findings would be recorded and cataloged for teacher training division, which would cultivate the future faculty. The research and testing is part of graduate studies led by current faculty. At any rate, the system is capable of self-sustaining as each department feeds another, and self-replicating as the system cultivates its future generations. The accompanying drawings in the set show the system's expansion capacity, and a future projection of it taking over a larger territory. The May 1967 issue of *Arts & Architecture* featured the division and expansion drawings to demonstrate the extent of the structural revolution Wachsmann's proposal posed, however its ambition and contradictions are best seen in the carefully inked, and partially colored final drawing of the set that show the system expanded to include "the society of man."

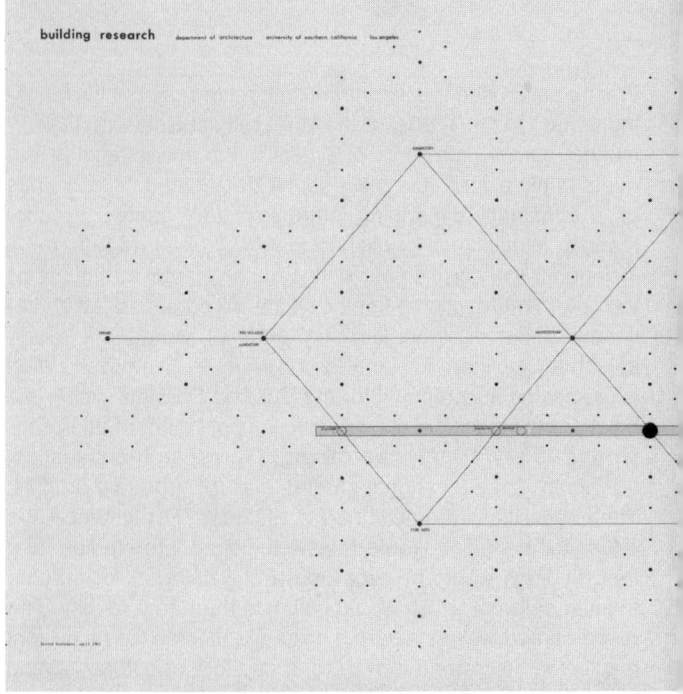

● "Coordination of Educational Information" drawing
showing the "linear evolution in education in the
complex pattern of learning."

chart 1

COORDINATION of EDUCATIONAL INFORMATION

linear evolution in education in
the complex pattern of learning

The design of a building process and its components are key topics in Konrad Wachsmann's work. His focus on the unfinished house, on constructive elements, instead of iconic buildings, heralds a turning point, both in building and in architectural thinking, where the creation of architecture is no longer related to the design of a building only. He reminds us that modern buildings are not just holistic entities but that they are made out of many researched and developed components that have a long history of failure and success.

● Presentation of the first Packaged House in Somerville, Massachusetts, in a warehouse owned by the U.S. Plywood Corporation in 1943.

"The Packaged Exhibition": A photograph taken at the presentation of the first Packaged House System in Somerville, Massachusetts in February 1943, captures a building process and became a reference point for the exhibition design. The photograph shows five men assembling or disassembling the prefabricated elements of the housing system using only hammers. It depicts the unfinished, the process of building, a dynamic act that implements time and movement and demonstrates the used technology. The set up of our exhibition is based on this moment in the process. Its open system and simple construction allow the exhibition to grow and to adapt to various places through new configurations.

The system builds upon Wachsmann's modular grid, which he developed for the General Panel System, and consists of only two simple elements: a frame, that holds the information panels, and a connecting element made out of a simple threaded rod. Neither screws nor other mechanic connections are needed for installation. It is a network of research, ready to be shipped around the world.

● The prefabricated exhibition system at the Bauhaus in 2018.

Teamwork: The detailed design of processes appears in Konrad Wachsmann's building research as well as in his teaching method. Process-oriented teamwork and interdisciplinary exchange were characteristic of Wachsmann's teaching. For his "Wachsmann Seminars," that he held around the globe, he developed a teamwork-system, a collaborative pedagogy, that entailed the destruction of authorship and questioned the production of architecture in his time.

This research is a product of the interdisciplinary group work that took place as part of the Bauhaus Lab. For three months, eight participants, from all over the world, with different professional backgrounds explored Konrad Wachsmann's "Art of Joining" in its socio-political context.

● Installation of the prefabricated exhibition system at the Bauhaus in 2018.

● Collage, Bauhaus Lab 2018.

We consider Wachsmann's pedagogy and our collaborative curating to be similarly complex processes that interweave diverse knowledge to create a dense network of research. It is the product of constant re-reading, adding, mixing, assembling and disassembling of contents into one multi-layered body of work. During this process visual techniques such as collective collages, writing and model building were important languages used to formulate a common thought.

Exhibition

Photographs of the finished exhibition and installation,
as well as photographs of our meetings and work process.

... PRICE ...

FERAL...

ISOZAKI

NATALINI

PLUS...

LASDUN

AO LONDON architects show A+P SMITHSON

THE VENTURIS COLIN ROWE

...RT NET LONDON JULY 5—14 1976

...round the ... Salzburg ...), University ...) and ...he U.S. ...59), students ...act Wachs- ...adigm. He ...s to manage ...d in Tokyo ...udents ...ps of three ...ected to ...a collective ...gress every ...as scheduled

to finish in three weeks; yet it lasted two months. Wachsmann's global teaching practice was part of a greater set of practices and policies employed by U.S. to affect the post-war reconstruction. An illustration describing the Japan worshop published in "Sinkentiku" depicts Wachsmann dropped like a paratrooper, alluding to his role as part of the cultural bureaucracy. Even after the end of his sponsored tour, Wachsmann kept travelling to deliver lectures around the world. He used his exhibits and lectures as opportunities to expand his network.

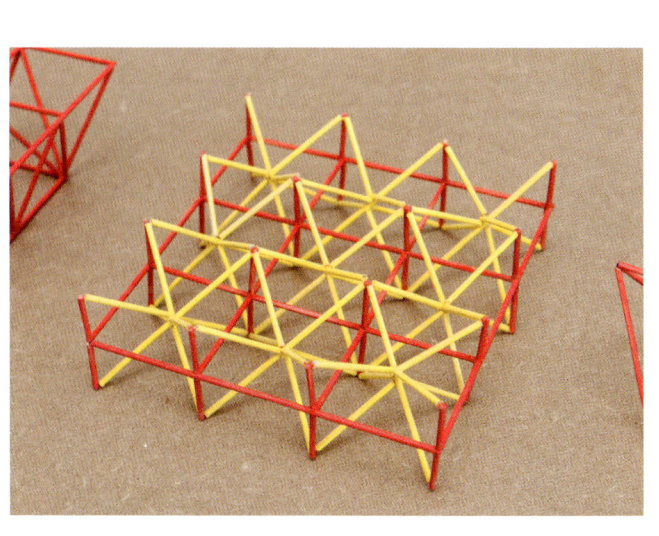

Appendix

The Art of Joining:
Designing the Universal Connector
A symposium held at the Bauhaus Dessau, August 9, 2018

Is there a universal architecture of systems that change the very idea of building, which essentially is a matter of defying gravity, to a matter of omitting it? Konrad Wachsmann`s universal wedge connector, invented in the shadow of the world war, and applied in the General Panel System in collaboration with Walter Gropius in the U.S. in 1941, was the point of departure of the Bauhaus Lab 2018. The postgraduate program is part of the Bauhaus Dessau annual theme of "standard"—a perspective on Bauhaus historiography that focuses on the search for modular systems and types in response to the rationalization processes in the 20th century. Himself an immigrant, Wachsmann`s alignment with rationalization and standardization, applicable in diverse contexts and conditions, shared the ambiguities of modern architecture and its claim for universality. Like virtually no other modern architect, Wachsmann advanced the industrialization of architecture and the associated possibilities of a turning point in architecture. The universal combinatorics and maximum flexibility of the prefabricated connectors had the potential to make everyone a designer of the built environment.

The international participants of the Bauhaus Lab 2018 investigated the historical context and discourses of transatlantic postwar modernism bundled in the metal connector. The three-month-long research, which included excursions for on-site investigation and archival study, culminates in an exhibition in the Bauhaus building. Its grid system juxtaposes the virtual three-dimensional grid that General Panel System inscribed in space with the DIN norms, the contemporary paragon of standardization. The findings are displayed in thematic chapters, revolving around different spatial constellations the connector brought together. The exhibition opening on 9 August 2018 was accompanied by an international symposium in which the participants of the program and invited scholars and architects updated the architectural discourse that surrounded the "universal connector."

In three round tables the participants of the Bauhaus Lab discussed with Georg Vrachliotis (Karlsruhe), Suzanne Strum (Barcelona) Christian Sumi (Zurich) and Douglas Murphy (London) the architecture of systems, the contested legacy of prefabrication, and the topicality of the "turning point of building."

● *1 Roundtable*

The Architecture of Systems
Introduction—Regina Bittner
Statements—Georg Vrachliotis, Suzanne Strum
Discussion—with the Bauhaus Lab participants

12.30-1.30 pm

Lunchbreak

1.30-3.00 pm

● *2 Roundtable*

The contested legacy of prefabrication
Statement—Douglas Murphy
Discussion—with the Bauhaus Lab participants

3.00-4.00 pm

● *3 Roundtable*

The topicality of the "turning point of building"
Statemenr—Christian Sumi
Discussion—with the Bauhaus Lab participants

● *Elizabeth Andrzejewski* is a designer and maker trained in architecture. She is completing her master's degree in architecture at Pennsylvania State University, where she researches metal fabrication, building methods, and the universal joint.

● *Phillip Denny* is an architecture writer and historian. He is currently a PhD student at Harvard University, where his research focuses on media and architecture history from the postwar to the postmodern.

● *Rhiannon Haycock* is a researcher based in London. Her research focus includes participatory design and innovation, redistributed manufacturing and material culture.

● *Ezgi Isbilen* is a PhD candidate at Virginia Tech. She studies architecture's complex relationships with its modes of production, and the discourse of construction in the 20thcentury.

● *Eva-Maria Offermann* is a German designer whose work is based on concepts shifting between art and design—searching to find out what exactly that means. She started her studio in 2012, focusing on printed matter, while exploring the possibilities of systems.

● *Adam Przywara* is a PhD candidate in the Manchester Architecture Research Group, University of Manchester. His research engages with historical and contemporary entanglements between architectural materialities, war and capitalist development.

● *Daniel Springer* is an architectural designer and researcher based in Berlin. In addition to his collaborative practice, he is currently researching and teaching at the HafenCity University in Hamburg with a focus on cultural production at the intersection of architecture and art.

● *Lisi Zeininger* is an architect based in Vienna. Her previous work focused on architectural concepts and realizations of public, cultural, and educational buildings.

● Acknowledgement
Team Academy Bauhaus Dessau Foundation:
Head of the program: Dr. Regina Bittner,
Research associate: Philipp Sack

Art Study Center, Harvard Art Museums (Cambridge MA),
Eva Babatz (Bauhaus-Archiv, Berlin), Dr. Eva-Maria Bark-
hofen, Tanja Morgenstern, Juliane Kreißl (Baukunstarchiv,
Akademie der Künste, Berlin), Franca López Barbera, Alison
Cain-Fukuchi, Adam Strohm (Paul V. Galvin Library, Univer-
sity Archives and Special Collections, Illinois Institute of
Technology, Chicago), Torsten Ceglarek (Dessauer Verkehrs
GmbH), Sebastian Czerny (Stiftung Bauhaus Dessau), Kate
Donovan (Houghton Library, Harvard University, Cambridge
MA), Wendy Hubbard (Gropius House, Lincoln MA), Prof.
Dr. Joachim Krausse (Fachhochschule Anhalt, Dessau), Dr.
Martin Mäntele (HfG-Archiv, Ulm), Nathaniel Parks (Ryerson
& Burnham Archives, Art Institute Chicago), National Mu-
seum of American History, Katrin Schenk (Stiftung Haus
Schminke, Löbau), Smithsonian Institution, Ray Wachsmann,
Claudia Wieltsch (Konrad-Wachsmann-Haus, Niesky), René
Wollschläger (Stiftung Bauhaus Dessau), Ines Zaluendo,
Johanna Kasubowski (Frances Loeb Library, Harvard GSD,
Cambridge MA), Dr. Michael Zinganel (Wien), Henning
Seilkopf & Holger Ziolkowski (Stiftung Bauhaus Dessau)

● Bauhaus Taschenbuch 23
The book is published in conjunction with the Bauhaus symposium *The Art of Joining: Designing the Universal Connector* held at the Bauhaus Dessau, August 9, 2018 at the Bauhaus Dessau Foundation.

● Edited by
Bauhaus Dessau Foundation
Director Claudia Perren
Gropiusallee 38
06846 Dessau-Roßlau
Telephone +49-340-6508-250
www.bauhaus-dessau.de

● Editing
Phillip Denny, Adam Przywara

● Proofreading and Translation
Bauhaus Lab 2018,
Mary Lynch-Lloyd ("Just Structures in Space")

● Project management
Katja Klaus

● Graphic design
Anne Meyer
based on a concept by HORT, Berlin
www.hort.org.uk

● Printed by
Pöge Druck, Leipzig
www.poegedruck.de

● Publisher
Spector Books, Leipzig
www.spectorbooks.com

● Distribution
Germany, Austria: GVA, Gemeinsame Verlagsauslieferung
Göttingen GmbH & Co. KG,
www.gva-verlage.de
Switzerland: AVA Verlagsauslieferung AG, www.ava.ch
France, Belgium: Interart Paris, www.interart.fr
UK: Central Books Ltd, www.centralbooks.com
USA, Canada, Central and South America, Africa, Asia:
ARTBOOK | D.A.P. www.artbook.com

First edition, 2019
© Bauhaus Dessau Foundation

ISBN 978-3-95905-284-9

The Bauhaus Dessau Foundation is a non-profit foundation under public law. It is institutionally funded by:

Die Beauftragte der Bundesregierung für Kultur und Medien

SACHSEN-ANHALT

Dessau
⌐ Roßlau

- p. 20, 22, 24, 25, 27, 28
Evolution of the Wedge Connector.

- p. 34
Richard Neutra. House design for General Paneral
System, circa Nov 1944.
© AdK Berlin

- p. 37
General Panel System Catalogue, 1946.
© Bauhaus Foundation, Dessau.

- p. 39
Thousand Lanes. Spring – Summer 1959.
© Bauhaus Foundation, Dessau.

- p. 40, 41, 42, 43
General Panel System. Catalogue, 1946.
© Bauhaus Foundation, Dessau

- p. 47, 48, 50, 53, 54, 55
© Museum Niesky, Konrad-Wachsmann-Haus Niesky
Goethestraße 2, 02906 Niesky.

- p. 59
U.S. Patent No.308,833, issued December 2, 1884.

- p. 64
© Bauhaus Archiv Berlin.

- p. 69
Courtesy of John Bollinger.

- p. 72, 73
Akademie der Künste, Berlin,
© Konrad Wachsmann Archive, Sig: Wachsmann 180.

- p. 74
Courtesy of John Bollinger.

- p. 77
"Memos, Wachsmann" in: *Crombie Taylor Papers,*
Ryerson & Burnham Archives, Art Institute of Chicago.

- p. 79
Courtesy of John Bollinger.

- p. 82
Courtesy of John Bollinger.

- p. 88
© Akademie der Künste, Berlin,
Konrad Wachsmann Archive, Sig: Wachsmann 2297.

- p. 94 – 97
© HfG-Archiv / Museum Ulm

- p. 101, 102
© University Archives and Special Collections, Paul V.
Galvin Library, Illinois Institute of Technology.

● p. 98 –100, 103 – 105
© Akademie der Künste, Berlin,
Konrad Wachsmann Archive.

● p. 106
Konrad Wachsmann, *Wendepunkt im Bauen*
(Wiesbaden: Krausskopf-Verlag, 1959), 56–57.

● p. 108, 109
Konrad Wachsmann, *Wendepunkt im Bauen*
(Wiesbaden: Krausskopf-Verlag, 1959), 58–59.

● p. 111
Akademie der Künste, Berlin,
Konrad Wachsmann Archive, Sig: Wachsmann 298.

● p. 113
Hendrik A. Kramers and Helge Holst, *The Atom and the
Bohr theory of its structure,* transl. R. B. Lindsay and
Rachel T. Lindsay, with a foreword by Sir Ernest Rutherford
(London: Gyldendal, 1923), chart without page number.

● p. 114
William F. Meggers: *Key to Periodic Chart of the Atoms,*
chart originally designed by Henry D. Hubbard in 1924
(Chicago: W. M. Welch Scientific Company, 1953).

● p. 115
H. E. White, "Pictorial representations of the electron cloud
for hydrogen-like atoms," *Physical Review 37,* (June 1931): 1416.

- p. 118
Elizabeth Andrzejewski and Eva-Maria Offermann:
Re-Drawing of diagram No. 75, Dessau 2018.

- p. 119
Akademie der Künste, Berlin, Konrad Wachsmann Archive,
Sig: Wachsmann 186.

- p. 121
Internationale Sommerakademie Salzburg, Seminar Bau:
*Kulturzentrum für kleinere Orte, in dem Wechselausstel-
lungen von Werken der Kunst, Wissenschaft und Technik
in originaler Größe und Farbe mit mechanischen Mitteln
wie Diapositiv, Film, Tonband vermittelt wird,* 1958,
Akademie der Künste, Berlin, Konrad Wachsmann Archive,
Sig: Wachsmann 189.

- p. 122
Akademie der Künste, Berlin, Konrad Wachsmann Archive,
Sig: Wachsmann 226.

- p. 123
Akademie der Künste, Berlin, Konrad Wachsmann Archive,
Sig: Wachsmann 186.

Internationale Sommerakademie Salzburg, Seminar Bau:
Hochhaus aus vorfabrizierten Leichtmetallelementen,
1960, Akademie der Künste, Berlin, Konrad Wachsmann
Archive, Sig: Wachsmann 191.

- p. 145
© Bauhaus Archiv Berlin

- p. 147, 149, 150
Bauhaus Lab 2018

- Front page
© Akademie der Künste Berlin, Konrad Wachsmann
Archive, Wachsmann 84.

- Exhibition photos
© Bauhaus Dessau Foundation

- Bauhaus Taschenbuch 2
Architektur aus der Schuhbox.
Baťas internationale Fabrikstädte

- Bauhaus Taschenbuch 3
Kibbuz und Bauhaus. Pioniere des Kollektivs

- Bauhaus Taschenbuch 5
Das Bauhausgebäude in Dessau
The Bauhaus building in Dessau

- Bauhaus Taschenbuch 6
Vom Bauhaus nach Palästina.
Chanan Frenkel, Ricarda und Heinz Schwerin

- Bauhaus Taschenbuch 7
Die Siedlung Dessau-Törten 1926 bis 1931

- Bauhaus Taschenbuch 9
Die unsichtbare Bauhausstadt. Eine Spurensuche
in Dessau

- Bauhaus Taschenbuch 11
Junges Design am Bauhaus Dessau

- Bauhaus Taschenbuch 12
Bauhaus Lab 2013. Architecture after speculation

- Bauhaus Taschenbuch 14
Die Werkbundsiedlung Stuttgart Weissenhof

● Bauhaus Taschenbuch 16
Die Dessauer Bauhausbauten

● Bauhaus Taschenbuch 17
Junges Design in den Meisterhäusern

● Bauhaus Taschenbuch 19
Mobilitätsdesign

● Bauhaus Taschenbuch 20
Desk in Exile: A Bauhaus Object Traversing
Different Modernities

● Bauhaus Taschenbuch 21
Bauhaus World Heritage Site

● Bauhaus Taschenbuch 22
Between Chairs.
Design Pedagogies in Transcultural Dialogue

Order in any bookstore or online
www.bauhaus-dessau.de